Rescue

*Abducted and threatened with death,
this woman and her husband draw on
God's lessons of a lifetime.*

Jean Phillips

Hannibal Books
P.O. Box 461592
Garland, Texas 75046

To order more copies
of *Rescue*

Contact:
Hannibal Books
P.O. Box 461592
Garland, Texas 75046

Fax: 1-972-487-7960
Phone: 1-800-747-0738
Email: hannibalbooks@earthlink.net
Visit: www.hannibalbooks.com

Order forms in back of this book.

Library of Congress Control Number: 2001099304
ISBN 0-929292-89-8

Dedicated

to

my beloved husband, Gene,
who has shared these experiences with me,
whose differences have added real spice to my life,
whose sense of humor has often made
me laugh when I wanted to cry,
and whose godly leadership and wisdom has kept us on track
for these 49 years of marriage;

to

Southern Baptists,
who had a part in our ministry
by supporting us through prayer and money,

and to

our children and grandchildren, so we can
" . . . tell the next generation the praiseworthy
deeds of the Lord,
his power, and the wonders he has done . . . and they in turn
would tell their children.
Then they would put their trust in God . . .."
Thus, "from generation to generation
we will recount (the Lord's) praise"
—*Psalm 78:4-7; 79:13.*

TABLE OF CONTENTS

Acknowledgements

In February 2000, while preparing to lead a week's study of *Experiencing God: Knowing and Doing the Will of God*, I read these words: "What are you attempting to do that only will happen if God brings it to pass?"[1]. As I meditated on this, the Lord reminded me of His leading me to write a book, but I'd been saying I didn't know how. That morning I told Him, "This is something I can't do. I don't have the ability, Lord, but You do. If You want me to write a book, I will attempt it in Your power."

Therefore, I'm indebted to Dr. Henry Blackaby for letting God use him through his book to inspire me to get started. And I'm full of praise to my Lord for giving me inspiration, wisdom, courage, creativity, and perseverance to see it through to the end. Many of the ideas and verses occurred to me during my Quiet Time as God spoke to me. I'm also indebted to the group that asked me to lead the *Experiencing God* study.

My deepest gratitude goes to my husband, Gene, who has helped in every step of the writing. He often refreshed my memory, suggested stories to include, prayed with and for me as I wrote, read and reread the manuscript to give corrections and advice, and was very patient during the long hours I spent at the computer.

I would also like to thank our sons, Mark and Paul, for coaching me into the world of computers when I thought I was too old to

8

learn. My gratitude also goes to Mark and son John for allowing me to tell their very personal experiences in this book.

I'm grateful for Gene's mother and my mother, both of whom are with the Lord now, and to our daughter, Beth, who saved our letters through the years. These letters, dating back to 1956, were highly helpful in my writing.

Thanks also to our son-in-law, Wes Gestring, and missionary co-workers who read parts of the manuscript to give suggestions.

A big thanks goes to John for giving permission to use his animal drawings at the beginning of each chapter.

I am most indebted to my dear friend, Joan Inabinet, from First Baptist Church, Camden, SC, for reading the manuscript in its early stages and offering invaluable advice and encouragement. Her candid observations helped me clarify many obscurities in the story.

Last, to my editors, Louis and Kay Moore, I give my deepest gratitude. Through Hannibal Books they provided me, an inexperienced writer, with a chance to be heard. They patiently worked with me to see the book to completion. Thank you, Louis and Kay, from the depths of my heart.

—Jean Phillips
January, 2002

---

[1]Henry Blackaby, *Experiencing God: Knowing and Doing the Will of God* (Nashville: LifeWay Press, 1990), 118.

Foreword

Many readers will think, in reading *Rescue,* that the author has put together a composite of experiences from a multitude of missionaries. However, the flow of narratives in this book reflects the pilgrimage of Gene and Jean Phillips through a lifetime of missionary service in Africa.

Family crises, robberies, tragic accidents, isolation, and threats throughout an era of war and violence are only a precursor to their being abducted and almost losing their lives during a post-retirement, short-term assignment in Lesotho.

Through it all, the Phillipses are sensitive to what God was teaching them, using every trial to grow in faith. Now they can celebrate a lifetime of service in a testimony to God's faithfulness. It is a blessing to see how Jean Phillips' passion for God's glory and to make Him known superceded and brought victory in the trials and challenges.

Missionaries will be able to identify with the cost of God's call to overseas ministry and adjustments, but every reader will be blessed and challenged to a deeper walk with God and to see every trial as an opportunity to glorify Him.

Jerry A. Rankin, President
International Mission Board
Southern Baptist Convention

PREFACE

"We are hard pressed on every side, but not crushed;
perplexed, but not in despair; . . . struck down, but not
destroyed . . . so that the life of Jesus may also be revealed in our
body"
—2 Corinthians 4:8-10.

"And we, who with unveiled faces all reflect the Lord's glory,
are being transformed into his likeness with ever-increasing
glory . . . "
"until the day breaks and the shadows flee . . ."
—2 Corinthians 3:18; Song of Songs 4:6.

At the end of long, scorching hot days of ministry while living on the Sasame mission station in rural Gokwe, Zimbabwe, Africa, my husband Gene and I at sundown enjoyed walking with our dogs. As we trekked down the mission airstrip, we welcomed the cool breezes. As the sun dropped beyond the horizon, we delighted in watching the moon appear in its splendor. Sometimes it was only a sliver. On nights when it was full, we watched it cast long shadows on our pathway. And by its light, we found our way home in the dark. At other times, clouds hid its brightness from us, and we groped our way home in the darkness.

Like the moon, our lives reflect the greater light of the Son. Sometimes, we shine only as a sliver. At other times, our light is hidden by sin. But when our fellowship with the Lord is sweet and unhindered, we're full moons. Often when He's shining brightest on our life, deep shadows are cast in our pathway. In the midst of the shadows of pain, disappointments, danger, and heartache, my husband and I have experienced God's presence and His grace. We've come to know Him better and to fellowship with Him in His sufferings.

As you read about our experiences, especially those in which God literally rescued us while we were walking through some of the deepest, darkest shadows in our life, we pray that you will be pointed to Jesus—the Light of the world. Our prayer is that you will allow Him to light up the dark places of your life so you can shine with His light in this world of darkness.

MOON SHADOWS

A pilgrim I in this dark world of shadows and of night—
Here, like the moon, Lord, let me shine with your Son's brilliant light.
Help me not gaze at shadows dark but keep my eyes above
By trusting in your faithfulness and love.

In pilgrim land, I want to shine on people lost in sin;
No hope have they when shadows come, no peace nor light within.
Revive us, Lord, that we Your church in trials sore may shine
And show the world Your wondrous light divine.

Moon shadows, that fall in darkest night—
Moon shadows, with naught to hide the light—
Moon shadows, reflecting God's dear Son—
Lord, may I shine until You call me home.

—Jean Phillips
December, 2000

PART 1

THE JOURNEY'S END?

"They will still bear fruit in old age, they will stay fresh and green, proclaiming,
'The Lord is upright; he is my Rock, and there is no wickedness in him'"

—Psalm 92:14-15.

14

Chapter 1

Staring Death in the Face

" . . . I consider my life worth nothing to me, if only I may finish
the race and complete the task the Lord Jesus has given me—the
task of testifying to the gospel of God's grace"
—Acts 20:24.

"Unless the Lord had given me help, I would soon have dwelt
in the silence of death"
—Psalm 94:17.

Rousing from a deep slumber, I heard the bedroom door open.
My first thought was that Gene had stirred from sleep and was moving about the room. I began drifting back to my sleepy state, but
when I turned over, I realized Gene was still beside me. Then who
had opened the door?

In the darkness, illumined only by the glow of the full moon
piercing through the skylight in our bedroom, I wakened further.
My blurry eyes made out the form of a man standing beside our

bed. Immediately I saw other men slipping through the bedroom
door and joining him in the room.

Still groggy, I thought, *They've come from David, our landlord,
to give us a message. But how did they get in the house?*

The words I heard next jarred me fully awake. "Hands up!"
commanded one of the men.

I realized Gene was now also alert and at attention. He saw the
silhouettes of five men standing about us. Lying there in bed, at
their command, we both put our hands above our heads. I began to
pray quietly, "Lord, take care of us." Then, sensing an evil presence
in the room, under my breath I said, "Jesus, I ask you here and now
to bind Satan."

"We're not planning to hurt you," one of the men said, clearly
lying. "We just want your money and your car keys."

We couldn't see their faces in the dark; only their forms were
visible. For all we knew, they could have had on ski masks. Some
also appeared to be wearing a type of jumpsuit or work uniform.

Still lying in bed, Gene answered with a calm and gentle voice,
"We'll give you anything you want."

* * * * *

Having retired from 40 years of active mission service in
Zimbabwe with the International Mission Board of the Southern
Baptist Convention, Gene and I were now on a volunteer stint in
Lesotho, Africa[1]. It was about 2 a.m. February 1, 1999. We had
arrived in Lesotho six weeks earlier and were there to work with
Southern Baptist missionaries Charles and Rebecca Middleton.
Living in the quiet village of Morija, we were 45 minutes from the
capital city of Maseru, where the Middletons lived, and about 40
minutes from the university town of Roma, where our daughter,
Beth, and her husband, Wes Gestring, along with their three children, served with Campus Crusade for Christ.

Landing in Johannesburg, South Africa, on September 15, 1998,
we had intended to go directly to Lesotho and serve until mid-July
1999. Then we planned to spend another six weeks of ministry in
Zimbabwe. Because the results of recent elections were being con-
tested by the opposition party, political unrest was escalating in

Lesotho when we arrived. Shops were looted and burned, law and order had broken down, and missionaries were evacuating to Johannesburg. Consequently, this was not the time for us to go into Lesotho. Since roads were unsafe, and Wes and Beth and their family lived 45 minutes from the border of South Africa, they had to wait for a South African military convoy to evacuate them and other university personnel from Roma. Once safely out of Lesotho, they joined us in Johannesburg.

Since it was impossible for us to minister in Lesotho at that time, we headed north to Zimbabwe on October 1 where arrangements had been made for us to work with Dr. Maurice and Shirley Randall at the Sanyati Baptist Mission Station. We were highly conscious of the truth of Proverbs 16:4 and 9: "The Lord works out everything for his own ends . . . In his heart a man plans his course, but the Lord determines his steps." Since we had chosen in advance to follow His will, we made the adjustment to follow this new path He opened up for us. God knew we were needed at Sanyati more desperately in October, when the Randalls were the only missionaries there, than we would be in July and August when they would have other reinforcements.

We quickly became busy working with the area pastors and their churches as well as on the mission station. We enjoyed the ministry God gave us there and rejoiced in the souls saved. By mid-December things had settled down in Lesotho and the workload had slackened in Zimbabwe, so we said our goodbyes and headed for Lesotho.

Finding a place for us to live proved quite difficult, but eventually the Middletons located a quaint little three-room cottage in the mountain village of Morija. Our historic cottage had been built in the late 1800's by missionaries of the Lesotho Evangelical Church (LEC) to show Africans how to build rectangular houses. It was constructed of indigenous stones, with mud-plastered walls on the inside. In recent years, David Hall, the son of another LEC missionary, had worked out an arrangement with the house's owner to fix it up and rent it out to tourists. He had added a thin layer of cement to the mud walls, a cement floor, a bath, and a ceiling with tin roof to replace the original thatched roof. The cottage was near the end of the narrow dirt road that wound up the side of the mountain and passed through the LEC mission station. The only two houses in our immediate neighborhood with running water were our landlord's and ours. David had a lovely chateau-type house at the end of the road, where he and his family came from Maseru on weekends to relax and ride their horses.

Driving up the mountain, we could see our Basotho neighbors washing their clothes and getting their clean water from wells near the road. Small drab unpainted houses made of cement blocks or stones dotted the hillside. Many of their tin roofs were secured, not with nails, but with stones laid around the perimeter of the roof. Children played in yards and along the road, while pigs, cows and horses were staked near the houses. Scattered over the hillside were massive, spiky agave aloes in bloom, with giant stems topped with spectacular feathery yellow flowers reaching for the sky.

Having lived so many years in the hot, dry lowveld (lowland) of Zimbabwe, we enjoyed Morija's altitude of 6,000 feet, wonderful mountain breezes, cool mornings and evenings and pleasant daytime temperatures. We arrived in summer to find lots of sunshine and plenty of rain without humidity. We also were quite cozy and comfortable in our little cottage with its gas refrigerator and stove and battery-powered light bulb in the main room, which served as our kitchen-dining-living room. On one side of the main room was our office-guest room, while on the other side was our bedroom. The bathroom opened into the main room. In the main room was a small anthracite heater for the cold days of winter, which began in May and continued into September. Because of its high altitude and its monarchical form of government, Lesotho is known not only as the Mountain Kingdom but also as the Switzerland of Africa, with some of its mountains snowcapped all year.

Charles assigned us to open Baptist work in another village, Thabana Mohlomi, about 90 minutes from Morija. During the last three weeks of January, we worked with a team of youth from a small Baptist church in Maseru in a tent revival at Thabana Mohlomi. They rented a one-room-house in which to live during these weeks, and we stayed in a tent once or twice each week when we went out to work with them in visitation, preaching, teaching, and showing the JESUS film. Eventually Charles provided a tiny house trailer where we were to stay during our overnight visits.

The village people were interested in our message, but because many had backgrounds in other church groups, they were suspicious of us. Many still practiced their traditional beliefs and rituals, including worship of their ancestors, along with Christianity. When we preached that Jesus is Lord and allows no rivals, few were willing to make that kind of commitment to Christ. But the love of Jesus and message of His Word eventually began to penetrate their hearts. By the end of the meeting, on Sunday, January 31, a few had surrendered to Christ as Lord. Charles and Rebecca joined us for the closing meeting. Then we took down the tent and loaded the equipment and team members into our Toyota Venture and Charles' double cab pick-up. In late afternoon we arrived home, gloriously tired, and ready for a good night's rest.

The vehicle the mission furnished us held 10 people, or fewer if we were carrying a projector and other equipment. Early on, our landlord had warned us that thieves were stealing Ventures, because they were used as taxis. He had installed simple burglar bars in our cottage and had made some suggestions about keeping the car safe.

Until the night of January 31, we had not taken the warnings seriously. Evidently thieves had indeed targeted our vehicle and had watched our comings and goings, planning their strategy for the break-in. That Sunday night, without our hearing them, they pried the burglar bars out of the cement of the tiny bathroom window, which wouldn't lock, and all climbed into the bathroom. We heard them only when they entered our bedroom.

* * * * *

As Gene raised up to go and get the money and car keys, which were in his pants pocket in the office, one of the men, whom I call Loudmouth, yelled, "Where are you going?" Then he slapped my husband back down onto the bed.

"I'm just going into the other room where the keys and money are," Gene answered.

Probably thinking Gene would go for a gun, he cursed and screamed, "If you try anything, we'll rape your wife," and refused to let Gene leave the bed.

Realizing I would be less of a threat to them than Gene, I said, "Let me go and get what you want."

The thieves agreed to this. They sent another of their group, whom I call Foulmouth, to follow closely along with me. Passing some of the other men, who had moved into the kitchen, I was very aware of my vulnerability and at the same time of God's presence. Groping through the darkness, I managed to locate Gene's pants with his billfold and keys. Foulmouth grabbed the pants from me and retrieved what they had asked for.

Meantime, in the bedroom Loudmouth kept asking Gene for money. Gene thought I hadn't been able to find it and convinced them to let him go and get it. When he got to the room where I was, my husband took the pants and found the billfold missing. I spoke up for all to hear, "Foulmouth has taken the money. He has it all." But Loudmouth kept demanding, "Money! Money!" He slapped Gene again, this time so hard that my husband fell down. The print of the man's hand stayed on Gene's face for three days.

Seeing Gene on the floor, I boldly screamed, "You've killed him! You've killed him!" I didn't really believe he was dead, because I remembered something Gene and I had agreed on long before this time. We had schemed that if we ever found ourselves abducted or in a similar situation, I would pretend to faint and he would pretend to have a heart attack.

Stunned, yet seeing that his pretense brought no helpful results, Gene finally got up. He told Loudmouth the equivalent of about $500 in U.S. money was in his wallet. (Since we lived far from the bank, on Friday he had drawn out enough money to pay our rent and other bills that we'd have to pay at the beginning of the month.) When the men heard how much money was in the billfold, they began excitedly talking together in Sesotho and stopped harassing Gene. Later my husband testified that when Loudmouth slapped him those two times and cursed and threatened him, he felt no desire to retaliate. Instead of anger, he felt a sense of calmness and gentleness. This was a miracle from God, because the natural reaction of a man is to hit back when someone hits him. Gene also testifies that he felt no fear throughout the whole ordeal, just the perfect peace of God. This peace which we both felt was a gift of God to us in our time of need.

While all this was happening, one of the men took the car keys and unlocked the car door, setting off the burglar alarm. This awoke our neighbor, Tseou, who worked for our landlord in our yard. At 2:15 a.m. Tseou got up and quietly stood at his fence to see what was going on at our house.

By then, the men had told us, "We're taking you with us."

"Please let us slip some clothes on over our nightclothes," we begged. "And let us get our shoes."

Since Gene's pants and shoes were accessible, it was simple to grant his request. But my clothes were in the bedroom. Therefore, they sent Foulmouth with me again to watch my every move. Standing in front of the wardrobe in the darkness, I reached for a dress with elastic in the waist that I could slip over my gown, while Foulmouth asked, "Where's your gun?"

Pulling the dress over my head, and stuffing socks and underwear down the front of my dress, I answered, "We don't have a gun." I'm sure he expected me to pull a gun on him. We knew what he didn't know: our safety was not in guns, but in the Lord.

I located my lace-up shoes but was having a hard time getting them on without socks. Meanwhile, the men grew impatient. They started yelling obscenities and spitting out threats, "We'll kill you! You better do what we say, or we'll rape you!" I was amazed at their good English, realizing that they must have some education, but at the same time wondering where they learned such a lewd vocabulary.

Foulmouth took me to the car and put me in the back, while another of our abductors pulled the bedspread off our bed, and brought out Gene. Before getting into the back with me, Gene showed them the delayed switch on the car to keep it from cutting off a few hundred yards down the road and perhaps causing more trouble for us. When he climbed in the back with me, they covered us both with the spread. However, when the men couldn't get the car started, they started cursing and swearing. Then they forced Gene into the driver's seat to help. They assigned Foulmouth to the very back with me, while the others occupied the two bench seats. Because of our awkward driveway, they let Gene maneuver the vehicle out.

Tseou, hiding in the bushes at the fence, heard the men curse Gene when he didn't manipulate the turn at the first try. He heard them scream in Sesotho, "We'll kill you!" Then seeing the car disappear down the road in the darkness, Tseou ran up the road to tell our landlord what he had seen and heard.

Normally David and his family went back to Maseru on Sunday afternoons so they could be there for work and school Monday morning. But this week, his wife and children went back and he stayed for some business in Morija the next day. God engineered that plan, since David had the only phone in our immediate neighborhood, except for our cell phone, which was inaccessible at the time.

Tseou awoke David, told him what had occurred, and ran with him down to our cottage. There they found that we indeed were both gone. David phoned the police, who didn't answer, and Charles. Charles called Wes and the American embassy as well as missionaries in South Africa, telling them to pray. Wes made some calls to the States, and a prayer chain was set in motion around the world while we were still in the car with the thieves.

We, of course, knew none of these happenings. We had no idea that anyone except the Lord knew we had been kidnapped.

Scrunched down in the back, covered by the quilt, I felt covered and surrounded by God's warmth, love, and protection. As our car rumbled over the bumpy road down the mountain, through the mission compound, and out onto the main road, God spoke to us: "Peace I leave with you, My peace I give you; not as the world gives do I give to you. Let not your heart be troubled, neither let it be afraid" (John 14:27 NKJV). He also reminded us throughout the whole episode, "For God has not given us a spirit of fear, but of power and of love and of a sound mind" (2 Tim. 1:7 NKJV).

Assured that God was with us, we felt filled with His peace, power, and boldness to witness of Him. Giving victory over fear, he assured us that we were not really in the hands of those young men who were boasting of all the terrible things they would do to us. We were in the hands of our Lord and Savior, Jesus Christ, who had the final say about what would happen to us.

"God loves you and wants you to know Him," I said to Foulmouth as he spat out all kinds of vulgarity. "God wants to deliver you from the life you are now living. Because of His great love for you, Jesus Christ died on the cross to save you from your sins so you can live forever with Him. He rose again and is alive today. He lives in my heart because I have repented of my sins and believed on Him as my Savior. He's in me and with me right now, and because of that I do not hate you for what you are doing to us. I want you to repent and become God's child and my brother in Christ."

He listened as I talked. The Holy Spirit was planting the gospel message in his heart.

Though we never got a good look at our abductors, we came to realize that they were very young men, some perhaps still in their late teens. I wondered about their families and how they got into this life of crime.

While I was talking to Foulmouth, Gene, now out of the driver's seat but still up front, talked to those in the front two seats. "We are American missionaries and have come here to help you and your people. This vehicle doesn't belong to us but to our Mission. It is used to take us and our Basotho brothers and sisters around your country to tell your people of Jesus, God's Son, who died on the cross to save all who will believe on Him."

Upon hearing that we are Americans, Loudmouth said, "I've been to Atlanta. In fact, we are the Lesotho Mafia."

Eventually, the car stopped and one of the men said to Gene, "Get out of the front seat. I want to put you in the back with your wife so that young man won't rape her." (We found out later that one of the men had, indeed, served time in prison for rape.)

With Gene by my side once again, both of us covered by the blanket, we joined hands and hearts and quietly prayed together. Gene now began telling Foulmouth about Jesus and His love for him. This young man seemed to listen to God's message of salvation. In between our conversations with him, we would quietly pray. When our voices grew quiet, those up front would ask, "Are you praying?" Then they would command, "Don't pray!" *Were they afraid of our prayers?* we wondered.

Foulmouth kept his hands under the quilt so he could hold onto our clasped hands. At one point, he began feeling of our watches and wedding rings. I prayed, "Lord, he can have our watches, but please don't let him take our wedding rings." Soon he demanded, "Take off your watches and give them to me." As we took them off and handed them to him, he seemed satisfied and didn't ask for anything more. Today, our rings are continual reminders not only of our love for each other but also of God's love and care for us.

By this point, we had been riding with the men almost an hour and were in mountains where we had never been previously. The men had crossed a muddy riverbed, turned around, and were headed in the direction from which we came. But because we were scrunched down with our heads covered, we were disoriented. Finally Foulmouth asked, "Do you know where you are?" Without waiting for an answer, he taunted, "You're high in the mountains of Lesotho. Don't you feel dizzy?"

As the car began backing up, one of them said, "OK, now is the time you're going to die."

I thought, perhaps they're going to kill us by pushing us over a cliff. But with calmness and assurance, I answered the man, "Well, if you kill us, we'll just go to be with Jesus." Gene said the same thing.

Into my mind flashed, "For to me to live is Christ, and to die is gain." " . . . absent from the body . . . present with the Lord" (Phil. 1:21 (KJV); 2 Cor. 5:8 (KJV). I had no fear, just perfect peace, and a glorious expectation that I would simply go to sleep and the next face I would see would be that of my Lord. My only prayer and concern was for our family that would be left behind.

"But we'll make you suffer first. We'll cut you up in little pieces and torment you before we kill you," our abductors taunted.

"We'll still just go to our home in heaven to be with Jesus," we answered with calm assurance. We found out through this experience that God will give peace when our time comes to die. We may have to suffer first, but He'll be with us each step of the way. We thought our time had come to meet our Lord, and, with peace in our hearts, we were ready for Him to receive us.

The next thing we knew, the car stopped and our abductors got out and told us to get out also. Gene saw one of them pick up a huge rock which he thought they would use to hit us in the head. Instead, the man threw it down, and then told us to go to the side of the road and sit down. One handed me the quilt; then all of them got back into our vehicle and drove away. Much to our relief and surprise, they had left the two of us alone in the mountains.

God had rescued us! And through this experience He had given these men an opportunity to hear of His love and salvation through Jesus. What they did with the message was up to them. God also answered a prayer I had prayed the week before. Since we hadn't found many opportunities to witness to our neighbors, I had prayed, "Lord, I want to watch to see what You are doing here in Morija. Bring people to us and us to them so they will come to know You." Wow! What an awesome answer!

After we thanked God for this deliverance, the next thing I did after the men drove away was to don the clothing I had tucked away down the front of my dress. Then we started walking in the direction from which we thought we had come, though the men had left in the other direction. With the full moon lighting our way and casting shadows behind us, we wandered down the winding mountain road and waded through muddy riverbeds, trying to find our way out of the mountains. At one point we saw lights on the road behind us in the direction from which the men had let us out of the car. Thinking that perhaps our abductors were coming back to finish their job, we sought shelter in a cornfield. Rain had fallen earlier in the night, so it was wet and quite cool in spite of the quilt. After some time of lying or squatting in the field, I started becoming chilled. All this time, the light had not changed or moved. (This turned out to be the moon reflecting off the tin roof of a house.) At this point God reminded me of the last part of the verse we had been quoting, "For God hath not given us the spirit of fear, but . . . of a sound mind" 2 Tim. 1:7.

I said to Gene, "I think the sound mind God is giving us is to get up and get moving so we won't suffer from exposure. Let's trust Him to continue to take care of us as we walk."

We started walking again and soon passed through a village. Since we knew no one and couldn't speak the language, we didn't dare knock on a stranger's door in the middle of the night, so we passed on by. Continuing our journey, we waded through more rivers. We could see the outline of the mountains in front of us and noted that there seemed to be no break for a road to go through them. So we began to suspect that we were walking in the wrong direction and would not get home on this route. Still, there was nothing to do but keep on walking.

As dawn arrived, we encountered a man coming from his field.

He spoke no English, but we managed to use a bit of Sesotho mixed with our Zimbabwe Shona to make him understand that we needed help. He took us to the home of Mr. and Mrs. Ndaba, where the whole family of seven spoke English. They were Zulus.
Immediately we bonded with them because of the similarity of the Zulu language to Sindebele, another language spoken in Zimbabwe.

They were just awakening when we arrived. Before hearing our whole story, Mr. Ndaba welcomed us into their clean, comfortable home. Soon his wife joined us, gave us refreshing cups of hot tea, and listened to our story as she directed the children in their preparations for school. Next, our new friends located a neighbor who had a beat-up truck. The neighbor agreed to take us back to Morija. Mr. Ndaba insisted on accompanying us, riding in the truck's open back in the very cool morning air. Through this kind family, God wonderfully provided for our needs.

When we reached our home at 8 a.m., Wes, Charles and Rebecca, the American embassy staff, our neighbors, several branches of the police and others welcomed us, though amazed at our arrival in the truck. Not knowing anyone knew we had been abducted, we were overwhelmed at seeing the crowd. We embraced, cried, hugged some more, and began talking. Wes told of the prayer chains that had gone up for us. Others told of various rescue efforts that had been made throughout the night to try and locate us.

After we had talked with our friends, the police took our statements. As one finished taking mine, he turned to me and asked, "Why were you not killed? You said they kept threatening to kill you. They usually do in cases like this. So why didn't they kill you?" I answered, "We were not killed because people all over the world were praying for us, and our God answers prayer."

He turned back to his report and added these words: *"They were not killed because of prayer."*

In days to come, God continued to answer my prayer about witnessing. We told Tseou about the wonderful peace God had given us. We told him that we forgave our abductors and wanted to see them saved. He knew these young men since they were from Morija. He and the whole village were very ashamed at what they had done. He didn't understand why we said we didn't hate them but wanted them to know our Jesus. One day, a little later, he came to us and declared, "If your God can give you that kind of attitude and do all that for you, I want to be with you. I want to know your Jesus."

Tseou was a recovered alcoholic, but he had never accepted Jesus and knew very little of the things of the Lord. We told him the plan of salvation and gave him tracts and booklets to read. Then we gave him a Sesotho Bible. His wife was a backslidden member of another church and was steeped in ancestor worship. When Tseou was sick with a bad case of flu, we visited him and prayed for him. When he got well, he was full of gratitude to the Lord.

We began a Bible study in our home with Tseou, some of his family, and other neighbors who understood English. We hired a night guard, Peete, who also attended our Bible studies. Eventually Tseou, one of his sons, Peete, and others trusted Jesus as Savior. Others made fresh commitments of their lives to the Lord.

We rejoiced to know that Paul's words in Philippians 1:12 were true in our case, " . . . what has happened to (us) has really served to advance the gospel." Praise God for the truth of Romans 8:28 (KJV) that says, "And we know that all things work together for good to them that love God, to them who are the called according to his purpose".

We hadn't understood these truths in the beginning of our journey in missions years earlier in Rhodesia (Zimbabwe). But God used many and varied experiences to teach us.

---

[1] *Lethotho (leh-sue-two)* is the name of the country. *Basotho (bah-sue-two)* are the people. *Mosotho* (mo-sue-two) is one person. *Sesotho (seh-sue-two)* is the language the people speak.

PART 2

BEGINNING THE JOURNEY

" . . . *Leave your country, your people . . . and go to the land I will show you"*

—Genesis 12:1.

"You will go out in joy and be led forth in peace; the mountains and hills will burst into song before you, and all the trees of the field will clap their hands"

—Isaiah 55:12.

Chapter 2

Heeding the Call

" . . . I heard the voice of the Lord, saying, Whom shall I send, and who will go for us? Then said I, Here am I; send me"
—Isaiah 6:8 (KJV).

During the deep, dark days of the Depression, I made my entry into the world. I was born nearly nine months after the great stock market crash of 1929, on August 14, 1930, in Greensboro, NC.

My father, Eugene Jackson Jarvis, and my mother, Blanche Elizabeth Green Jarvis, were a May-December union. Daddy was 50 and Mama was 30 when I was born. I was Eugene's ninth and Blanche's first and only child. They named me Etta Eugenia and called me Jean.

Mama was Daddy's third wife. His first two wives as well as one of his children had died much earlier. Mama had attended Mars Hill College two years and had taught school, while Daddy, an expert cabinetmaker, had finished the third grade. Mama had been a good friend of the family for several years before Myrtle, Daddy's second wife, and mother of six of his children, died. Mama grieved with them over their loss. Later, when Daddy asked her to marry him, she took it as a calling from God and said, "Yes."

These were difficult years, not only for my family, but also for the nation. The Depression truly marred and altered the era of human history into which I was born. Before my birth, Daddy had lost his house and the little he had. We were poor, but everyone else seemed to be, too.

As the youngest of eight, I was doted on but not spoiled. As a young child, I learned to work in the fields and in the house. I don't remember any of us ever complaining about the work we had to do. At an early age I learned to cook and sew. When I was a teenager, I started making all my clothes. This was a step up from my four sisters' hand-me-downs I had always worn.

Mama and Daddy both loved the Lord with all their hearts and brought up their family in "the training and instruction of the Lord" (Eph. 6:4). Our lives centered around our Baptist church, where we heard fiery preaching and evangelistic zeal. Though Daddy had strict standards and we didn't have much money, we still had lots of fun. Mama played the piano and taught us all to sing and harmonize. At age 10, I joined the Jarvis "quartet", performing in singing conventions and churches. Mama also directed us in giving performances of Shakespeare and other dramas in our backyard.

Daddy was a deacon who brought many people to Jesus. He had a deep faith in God and in His Word. Often he was called on to pray for the sick. He took literally James 5:14-15, often anointing the sick with oil as he prayed for them. He reported that many were healed. A sickly child, I was the recipient of many of his prayers and anointings. I loved to hear my Daddy pray at church as well as in the home.

I do not remember a time when I didn't love Jesus. Some of my earliest memories are of snuggling up in bed with Mama while she made exciting Bible stories come to life for me. When I was 10, I publicly professed my faith in Christ and was baptized. However, one night when I was 12, while kneeling by my bed, God brought to my mind the words of Revelation 3:20 (KJV), "Behold, I stand at the door, and knock: if any man hear my voice, and open the door, I will come in to him, and will sup with him, and he with me."

I thought, "I believe in Jesus, but I don't ever remember opening the door and inviting Him to come into my life." So I prayed, "Lord Jesus, I believe you died for my sins and rose again. If I've never done it before, just now I open my heart to you and invite you to come into my heart." From that day forward, I never doubted my salvation. He came in when I invited Him, and I was God's child for eternity. (See John 1:12 and John 5:24.)

Mama said that as a young girl she thought God wanted her to be a missionary. Nevertheless, she found her mission field in rearing us children. All six of my half-siblings, who were at home when I was born, as well as I, made our professions of faith and sought to follow Christ fully. Spurgeon, the only non-Baptist, was faithful in his Methodist church. Dot became a nurse; Esther a pastor's wife and home missionary; and Bonnie a nursery worker in our home church and deacon's wife and mother of both a pastor and a pastor's wife. Carol and her husband served 37 years as missionaries in Venezuela, where one of their sons is now a missionary, and Wilbur, three and a half years older than I, was a faithful deacon. Mama and Daddy were truly faithful in the calling God gave them as parents.

When I was 14 I spent a week during the summer at Ridgecrest Baptist Assembly in North Carolina. It was there that I surrendered to do whatever God wanted me to do. Though I never told anyone at that time, I thought perhaps He wanted me to be a preacher's wife.

The next year, while at another summer camp, I first learned about the Spirit-filled life, yielded my all to Jesus, and asked Him to fill me with His Spirit. At that time, Galatians 2:20 became my life verse. "I have been crucified with Christ," was my affirmation. "I no longer live, but Christ lives in me." With wonder and amazement I'd repeat over and over, "Christ lives in ME."

Deeply in love with Jesus and gloriously happy in Him, I was ready to hear God's call to missions through studying His Word. I came to realize that without Jesus, people are condemned to an eternity in Hell. That included those in faraway lands who hadn't had the opportunity to hear the Gospel. One night I took personally the words in Ezekiel 3:17-18 and believed God had made me responsible for the lost of the world. I read that if I didn't warn the wicked to turn from their sins, when they died without Christ, their blood would be on my hands.

That night I dreamed about Judgment Day, when the nations of the earth will be gathered around God's great white throne. In my dream, I was standing next to that throne when an African man appeared before the Lord. God said to him, "Depart into everlasting fire, for you never knew me." Before going into the flames of hell, that man turned to me and said, "It's your fault. You didn't tell me about Jesus."

I awoke from that dream with tears streaming down my cheeks. I prayed, "Lord, I don't want it to be my fault that anyone goes to hell. I'll be your witness wherever I am, and I'll go where you want me to go." A few months later I publicly committed myself to missions and said, "Here am I, Lord. Send me."

In 1949, God led me to Mars Hill Baptist Junior College in the mountains of North Carolina. There I met a good-looking ministerial student who was also a football player. His name was Gene Phillips. Gene was from Woodruff, SC. His father, Paul, had been a supervisor in the cotton mill, where his mother, Lillian, also worked. Gene's brother, Henry, was 13 years older than Gene. His older sister had died when Gene was three. When she died, his father took his grief to the "bottle" and became an alcoholic, dying a tragic death when Gene was almost 16. But Gene's wonderful, Christian mother took her grief to the Lord and grew in Him. Through her strong trust in God, Gene was strengthened as he became the "man" of the house. He began working in the cotton mill each day after school and football practice.

Though his mother was Presbyterian, Gene attended the Baptist church near his home. Here, at age 10, he accepted Christ through the witness and concern of a Sunday School teacher. Then he heard and answered the call to preach when he was 16. Through much diligent work on his part and help from his church, God provided Gene a way to attend Mars Hill in 1948, the year before I arrived.

Could he be the preacher God had prepared for me? And was he also committed to missions? God had already taken care of that. The year before I met him, a missionary spoke in chapel at Mars Hill. God spoke through her to Gene. During the benediction, Gene quietly told God that if He wanted him on the mission field, he was willing to go.

Gene and I fell in love and began praying about God's will for

our lives. We were both interested in pioneer missions. My second
year, Gene transferred to Furman University in Greenville, SC.
During that year of 1950, Dr. Everett Gill of the Southern Baptist
Foreign Mission Board (now the International Mission Board) visited Mars Hill. I spoke with him about my interest in a pioneer mission field in Africa. He said, "Baptists are now in the process of
opening work in Southern Rhodesia." I shared with Gene the exciting things Dr. Gill told me.

During our courtship, people began referring to Gene and me as
the two "genes." At Mars Hill, Gene sang in the "Minister's
Quartet", and I sang in a girl's quartet. We combined the two groups
to make an octet and went on mission trips, where we witnessed
through song and sermon.

Gene and I were married in August, 1952. The saying that
opposites attract was certainly true with us. The first argument to
spoil our marital bliss occurred on our honeymoon. We were at our
"honeymoon cottage" in the mountains of North Carolina and
decided to visit some of the attractions around us. As we traveled,
Gene said, "Honey, let's go see Chimley Rock."

Thinking he had made a slip of the tongue, I said, "There's no
such place as Chimley Rock."

He assured me there was such a place. He had seen it. I argued,
"I've seen it too, but it's not Chimley Rock. It's Chimney."

"Nonsense," he said. "It's been Chimley all my life. Just wait
until we get to the sign, and you'll see how it's spelled."

After a few more miles we came to a sign that read, "See
Chimney Rock." I was quick to point it out to him, but he insisted,
"Well, what do you know? They've misspelled it."

We had a good laugh, but he admits that I won our first argument. He now says that I have been his "heavenly sandpaper" whom
God has used to rub off some of his rough edges. God also has used
him to chip away lots of corners in me that were unlike Jesus. Our
marriage has been exciting, yet challenging, because of our differences. But each time we've worked them out, we've grown closer to
each other and to the Lord.

In September, 1952, Gene entered Southeastern Seminary in
Wake Forest, NC, while I finished my last semester of college at
Woman's College of the University of North Carolina at Greensboro

(now UNC-G). In October, while still attending seminary, Gene was called as pastor of Southside Baptist Church in Greensboro. I joined him at Southeastern in January, 1953, and attended until our first child, Mark, was born in August, 1954.

Gene graduated from Southeastern in 1955 and continued to serve as pastor of Southside until the next year when we were appointed to Southern Rhodesia, later called Zimbabwe, as missionaries of the Southern Baptist Foreign Mission Board. We arrived in Rhodesia in October, 1956. Our journey in foreign missions had begun.

Chapter 3

Victory in Jesus

"Will you not revive us again, that your people may rejoice in you?"
—Psalm 85:6.

". . . Who will rescue me from this body of death? Thanks be to God—through Jesus Christ our Lord!"
—Romans 7:24-25.

The loud voices outside my bedroom window roused me from my afternoon nap. Eight months pregnant with our fourth child, I was exhausted from the heat as well as from grief over the recent death of my father. It was November, 1962—back in the days when missionaries didn't go home for funerals, so part of my grief was trying to comprehend the reality of the loss.

What I was hearing below was very real. My husband had taken a stand for truth when a pastor had received money through dishonesty. Now a delegation was at our house to confront Gene about the stand he had taken. In those days, Rhodesia seethed with much political and racial tension, and it boiled over into the church and our group of missionaries there. We received unkind, even threatening letters.

The last day of that month I rejoiced at the birth of baby Paul. Our other three children welcomed their new brother, while Gene and I thanked God for another healthy child to love and rear for Him. At 26 years of age, we had arrived as missionaries in Rhodesia with two-year-old Mark. John was born a year later, and Beth made her appearance in 1959. I had healthy pregnancies and loved the small government hospital in the asbestos mining town of Shabani, where we lived, and where each of the last three children was born. The same doctor delivered all three by natural childbirth.

During the months after Paul's birth, the political situation became worse. Southern Rhodesia, as it was called when we arrived, is a landlocked country in south central Africa. It is about the size of Montana, and English is its official language. The country boasts of the majestic Victoria Falls along its border with Zambia. Its altitude ranges all the way from its highest peak of 8,600 feet in the Eastern Highlands to its lowest point of 500 feet in the southeastern lowveld. Most of the country lies at more than 3,000 feet. It has a tropical climate that includes a rainy season during the summer months of November to April, when temperatures are quite comfortable on the central plateau but extremely hot in the lowveld. The dry season, from May through October, includes the mild winter months of May through August. During the winter, days are pleasantly warm and sunny, and nights are nippy with light frosts in much of the country and with heavy frosts in the highlands. The temperature builds up in September. The hottest time of year is October just before the rains begin.

The land's earliest settlers were the bushmen and Hottentots. Then came the Bantu. During the 1830's, the Ndebele, descendants of the Zulu, conquered the predominant Shona people and established a powerful kingdom.

The first British explorers arrived in the 1850s. They were searching for gold and ivory. Along with them came the colonists and missionaries. By 1897, the British had defeated the Ndebele and Shona people. The territory was called Rhodesia after explorer and colonist Cecil John Rhodes. An all-white legislature was then set up. In 1923, Southern Rhodesia became a self-governing British colony. Then in 1953, a federation was formed between Southern Rhodesia, Northern Rhodesia, and Nyasaland. In 1963, the federation broke up when the other two countries became independent nations with majority African rule. Northern Rhodesia became Zambia and Nyasaland became Malawi. Southern Rhodesia became known as Rhodesia. Because the whites in Rhodesia refused an African government, it remained a colony. This incensed the African majority, who had poor wages and living conditions as well as no right to vote. African political parties emerged, and the boiling kettle was preparing to erupt into civil war in the years to follow.

Our churches in Rhodesia felt the effects of political tensions. They weren't growing, and some seemed spiritually dead. At one point, molotov cocktails were thrown into church buildings, pastors' homes, and elsewhere. One night a pastor friend took refuge in our home because of threats of violence. I was filled with fear, discouragement, frustration, and disappointments. By 1964, as the time neared for our second furlough, I thought, "If we can just get to the States, I never want to return to Rhodesia."

Even at that, I dreaded furlough, for I kept thinking, "What will I tell the groups that ask me to speak? It seems all I've done these past two terms is have babies and take care of them. I love my God-called work as wife and mother, but who wants to hear about such mundane things?"

On the mission field to which God sent me, I became so consumed with my husband's and children's needs that I had forgotten my original commitments to my Lord. The revival I'd experienced at 16 years of age had faded, and I wasn't letting Christ live His life through me. Through busyness and neglect of a Quiet Time, when He could speak to me and I could talk with Him, His face had grown dim. I had lost the joy of my salvation. Gene and I both had been depending on methods more than on the Holy Spirit. We often grew impatient and unkind with each other, with the children, and with our co-workers. We were looking at circumstances rather than at the Lord.

The sad thing was that I didn't recognize my defeat. I was reading books on revival and, along with other missionaries, was praying for revival among our missionaries in Rhodesia and in our churches there. I focused on the need for renewal in others but not in me.

During that time, Dr. Sam and Ginny Cannata were on medical leave from Rhodesia because of an injury to one of Sam's eyes. While in the States, they met Bertha Smith, the legendary, retired missionary to China and Taiwan. God used her to help bring revival to their lives and to help them face victoriously the trauma of losing the sight in Sam's eye. They wrote us of their experiences and then invited "Miss Bertha", as people affectionately knew her, to visit Rhodesia.

Miss Bertha arrived in May, 1964, at the time of our mission meeting. (Back in those days, a mission meeting was when all the Southern Baptist Foreign Mission Board missionaries in a particular country got together for worship, mutual support, and business matters.) On meeting Miss Bertha, hearing her testimony and Bible teaching, and seeing her reliance on the Lord for everything, Gene and I began to long for a similar relationship with Jesus. We invited her to come to Shabani for meetings in our churches.

Soon after mission meeting, she visited us. This woman, who walked with the Lord, immediately perceived the heart of our need, and in her blunt, prophetic way began bursting our balloons of spiritual pride. She told us no revival would occur until God's people, beginning with us, were cleansed of sin. Then she urged us to get on our knees before the Lord with our Bibles, pen, and paper, and ask Him to show us our sin.

We began this personal "house-cleaning" rather reluctantly. But then, as we read God's Word and sought the Lord's face, we started seeing ourselves as God saw us. The result was first guilt, then repentance. As God showed me my sins, I wrote them down one by one—neglect of God's Word and prayer, anger, jealousy, impatience, unkindness, irritability, and wrong attitudes and motives. I recoiled at the ugliness of my heart as I saw my pride and selfishness, my self-will, self-righteousness, and self-centeredness. God also convicted me of the sins of criticism, complaining, ingratitude, worry, fear, and many other things.

Miss Bertha reminded us that when Jesus died on the cross, He took all our sins on Himself. He actually died in our place. So when He died, we died with Him. She urged us to confess as sin each thing God had shown us and not to excuse anything. If any of these sins were against a person, we were urged to make things right with him or her. Then we were by faith to put those sins on Jesus on the cross and receive His forgiveness. Next, we were to reckon ourselves dead to sin. We, by faith, were to see ourselves alive to Christ. We knew this is what our water baptism had pictured many years before. (See Rom. 6:4 and Col. 2:12.) After we had done all this, we were to tear up that sin list.

In the days following Miss Bertha's arrival at our place, we spent much time alone with the Lord. Our housekeeper, Rebecca Rupiya, took care of the children while God dealt with us. We had to go to each other and to our children and confess impatience, unkindness, and unfairness. We had to forgive each other. We also had to write some letters to make things right with others we had sinned against.

The Holy Spirit had come into our lives the moment we received Jesus years before (Rev. 3:20; Rom. 8:9). At that time, we were baptized by the Spirit into the body of Christ (1 Cor. 12:13). But because we had allowed self to control many areas of our lives, we were not Christ-controlled. We were not filled with the Spirit. Now, having confessed our sins and having been cleansed by the blood of Jesus, we were ready for a fresh infilling of God's Spirit.

I remember well the night when, with cleansed heart, I knelt and made a new commitment to the Lord. Through my tears I prayed, "Lord, I give you my hands, my feet, my lips, my voice, my mind, my thoughts, my heart, and my life. Live Your life through me, Jesus. I surrender to you my time, my talents, my money, and my plans—all I am and have. Father, I commit to you Gene and each of our children. I give you my family in the States. And Lord, I commit to You the churches and pastors, our work, the mission, and the political situation in Rhodesia. I choose Your will in advance for the future."

Thus surrendered, I took by faith the filling of the Holy Spirit to control every part of my life. God also dealt with Gene in these matters, and he, too, made a fresh surrender. Gene, too, was filled anew with the Spirit. We didn't have more of the Spirit now, but He had more of us!

I didn't hear any rushing sound from heaven; no strange

tongues came to me. But a deep joy and peace descended upon my soul, and I entered a new relationship with my Lord, with Him at the controls of my life. The next morning the birds seemed to sing more sweetly, the sky seemed bluer, and I wanted to sing and praise the Lord. Falling in love with Jesus all over again, I looked forward to meeting Him each day through the Word and prayer. The more I learned of Him, the more I wanted to know. Philippians 3:10 became my watchword, "I want to know Christ and the power of his resurrection and the fellowship of sharing in his sufferings, becoming like him in his death."

Miss Bertha led a prayer retreat, and many of our missionary co-workers experienced true revival. We had a greater love for each other and a better working relationship in the mission. We began to seek God's will instead of trying to push for our own agenda. We experienced new boldness and power in witnessing. Revival occurred more with us missionaries than to our churches at that time.

In the days ahead, we had to learn to walk in the Spirit and not in the flesh. Miss Bertha taught us to keep our sins forgiven up-to-date. When we slipped into the old ways, we learned to confess our sins and continue yielding to the Lord. We had to be continually filled with the Spirit. Gradually we learned to claim Christ's victory over those sins that seemed to have a grip on us. We also had to learn not to give any place in our lives to the devil but to resist him in every way. (See Gal. 5:16; Rom. 6:11-13; 1 John 1:7, 9; Eph. 5:18; and James 4:7-8 for the principles of victory this paragraph mentions.)

When time arrived for our second furlough, instead of dreading it, I looked forward to telling what God had done in our lives. I also looked forward to the time when we could return from furlough to Rhodesia where God had called us.

I had learned the source and principles of victory. Next, God was going to give me many opportunities to put them into practice. I was going to fall again and again, but each time, Jesus would pick me up, and we would walk on together to higher ground.

PART 3

GOD'S SCHOOL OF FAITH

"Endure hardship as discipline; God is treating you as sons."
—Hebrews 12:7.

Teach me, dear Lord, in your School of Faith,
Teach me to trust in Your Son;
Produce in me a harvest that's good
Through all the hardships that come.

Discipline me as Your child so dear;
Train me to believe Your Word.
May I leave doubts, self-pity, complaints;
Teach me the fear of the Lord.
                              —Jean Phillips

Chapter 4

Learning to Trust in God

" *'For I know the plans I have for you,' declares the Lord,*
'plans to prosper you and not to harm you, plans to give you hope
and a future'"
—Jeremiah 29:11.

"Trust in the Lord with all your heart and lean not on your own
understanding"
—Proverbs 3:5.

The dusty and bumpy gravel road wound through rocky out-crops of hills as we traveled deeper into the dry bush of the south-eastern lowveld of Rhodesia. The world around us looked drab and dead and spoke of months without rain. Fields and trees displayed evidence of recent bush fires that had sapped their last bit of beauty. After traveling 50 miles in these surroundings with the heat bearing down on us, we were tired and exhausted.

Suddenly we seemed to enter a fresh world of beauty. The road began stretching through acres and acres of bright green sugar cane fields. Our hot dusty car passed under a huge overhead sprinkler, busy watering the fields, and the fresh smell—like that of wet earth after a rain—was glorious. It was August 1964 just before furlough, and Gene was taking the children and me to visit the Triangle Sugar Estates, the "caneland" of Rhodesia.

Only a few decades earlier, this part of the country had been a wilderness. A few Africans from the Shangaan tribe lived there and eked out a living from snaring game and netting fish along the Mtilikwe and Lundi Rivers. Its low, unreliable rainfall—averaging about 18 inches annually, most of which fell between November and April—made farming a great chance. In some years as much as 40 inches of rain fell, but in other years only five inches occurred. Summer temperatures, often above 100 degrees Fahrenheit in the shade, also made this an undesirable area in which to live.

But in 1912, a young Scotsman named Murray McDougall arrived in the area and started a cattle ranch. Soon he dreamed of growing sugar cane there. He began working to make his dream come true. His first step was to build a small dam. For seven years, he and a handful of untrained African laborers worked to tunnel a waterway eight miles in length from the dam through granite hills to his fields. In 1935, he imported three lengths of cane, each three feet long. From this small beginning, his dream became reality.

In 1957, the Hulletts Organization from South Africa took over the project. By 1965, the company owned 212,000 acres in this area, with 31,000 acres under cultivation. The remainder of the land was used for cattle ranching. By a series of well-constructed dams and 42 miles of irrigation canals, formerly arid lands began to glow with cool green sugar cane. Citrus groves, banana and papaya trees, wheat and cotton fields, and acres of beans and maize were added. Their beauty and importance increased the productivity of the area. The company eventually had a completely Rhodesian directorate, and it began cattle ranching, cotton ginning, and production of animal feeds. Their large transport system moved over 1 million tons of cane to its sugar mill each season.

With all this development, people arrived searching for work and a better way of life. The neat houses, which Triangle provided for its employees, included green lawns, flowering trees, and shrubs. Workers soon planted gardens featuring flowers, vegetables, and fruits, which seemed to make the area's heat more tolerable.

Gene had first heard of this development, located 180 miles from Shabani, two years earlier. The 21,000 Africans and 1,000 Europeans (all whites were called Europeans) living on the Estate had no evangelical witness and were a great burden on his heart. In 1962 he started making monthly preaching trips to the area and then placed an African seminary student there to sell Bibles and preach during school holidays. Returning from each trip to Triangle, Gene told me about the challenge of the area. But I could not catch his enthusiasm until the children and I made this trip with him just before furlough in 1964. Once I saw it, I immediately adopted his vision, too. After the revival I'd experienced, I was ready to hear God speaking to me. Now both of us felt God leading us to move to the area, on our return from furlough, to strengthen this new work.

Furlough itself was wonderful! We saw my precious, widowed mother and other family members and friends and spoke in many churches, all the time learning more of our Lord. Toward the end of furlough, we learned some lessons about trusting God and accepting disappointments. About four weeks before we sailed on the Queen Mary for Southampton, England, to return to Africa, I pulled a muscle in my back. Wracked with pain, I lay in bed instead of attending all the events marking the end of our furlough. I visited a chiropractor several times before we left and then underwent physical therapy on board the ship. Because of that, I was feeling much better by the time we got to England. I was able to fly the rest of the way to Salisbury, Rhodesia, but we had to cancel our trip to Israel.

Other missionaries met us in Salisbury. As we walked together through the airport terminal, one of them said to Gene and me, "We haven't been able to find a place for you to live in Triangle."

Shocked and disappointed, yet clinging to the firm belief that God had called us there, I listened to their story of numerous failed attempts to locate a house for us. Then I blurted out these words: "I'm sure we'll find something once Gene can go and talk with the officials on the sugar estate."

Having no place to live was nothing new to us. In 1956, when we and our eldest child first arrived in Rhodesia, we had to reside with another missionary family until a house became available. But now, as a family of six, we faced a much more difficult dilemma.

Triangle was a private sugar estate and was still very new. It had no houses available for non-employees. Because of the political instability of the country, as well as other circumstances, the Mission did not believe that the time was right to build a house there. The previous year Ian Smith had become prime minister of Rhodesia. He had begun pressing Britain for independence. However, Britain's conditions of majority rule were not acceptable to Rhodesia's whites. So in November, 1965, Mr. Smith's government declared a Unilateral Declaration of Independence, which was declared illegal by Britain.

Missionary John Griggs, who lived in Fort Victoria, 110 miles from Triangle, had been negotiating with the sugar company to allow us to rent one of its houses until the Mission could build a house there. Before we had left the States, we had heard that a house would most likely be available by our arrival in Triangle.

So, when we landed in Harare, we expected to go directly to Triangle and the new work God had called us to do. Once we were informed of the obstacle of no housing, we committed the matter to the Lord, knowing that if He wanted us there, He would provide a place for us to live. Instead of the matter being resolved instantly, it actually became more difficult in the days and weeks ahead. God was at work using this situation to teach us some important lessons!

Vacationing friends in Fort Victoria offered us their apartment for three weeks. Leaving the family in the apartment, Gene made trips to Triangle to hunt for a place to live. After three weeks of searching, begging, and praying, all he was able to locate was a farmhouse 25 miles from Triangle over a rough dirt road full of corrugations and potholes.

Accepting this as God's provision, we enrolled Mark, John, and Beth in the Triangle school and moved into the farmhouse the day school started. As we made the hour-long trip from Triangle to our new home on Samba Ranch, every bump jarred my still-sore back, and our son Paul, only 2 1/2 then, threw up several times on the way. After an hour of travel on that road, the whole family was exhausted. Consequently, I slipped back into my old ways and questioned "Why, Lord? Why couldn't you get us a house in Triangle? It doesn't make sense for us to pass by all those thousands of lost people on the Triangle estates to go and live in a remote farmhouse where our nearest neighbor is a mile away."

As we arose each morning just after five o'clock to get the children ready for school that began at 7 a.m., Satan would ply me with questions and doubts. I would ask, "Why, Lord, did you put us way out here? Did you really call us to leave Shabani and the work there? Did we run ahead of you in coming here?" Then I'd whine, "It's not right for our little children to have to travel 50 miles round trip to school every day." My pity party was in full swing.

After kissing Gene and our three school children goodbye as they left each morning at 6 a.m., little Paul and I would go into the garden with my Bible and his toys. All around me I saw God's creations—the herd of impala that grazed in the field in front of our house, the noisy weaver birds as they built their nests in the huge mahogany tree with its dense shade, and busy ants hurrying to gather their food. I drank in the serenity of the rustic rocky hills surrounding the house and the beauty of the clear blue sky. I took joy from fluttering butterflies getting nectar from sweet-smelling flower blossoms. All of these spoke to me of God's loving care and mighty power. As I opened His Word each day, He began to teach me, and I began to listen.

One day I prayed, "Lord, you own the cattle on a thousand hills. You could have opened up a house for us in Triangle if that had been your will. Instead, you have put us here. Forgive me for complaining and for questioning you. Thank you for what you have provided. I'm available for you to use me right here where you've put us."

Gene joined me in thanking God for His provisions. And with that prayer and new attitude, I found peace and joy. Our circumstances didn't change. We did!

During our four months on Samba Ranch, we learned much. We found great joy in a simple lifestyle without frills or detractions. Because of my still-weak back, I seldom made the trip into town. Thus, during the mornings I found time to play with Paul, to focus my love and attentions on him and to teach him. I had time to help the children nurse back to health a wounded baby bird Paul had found one morning. In the afternoons and on weekends, Gene and I enjoyed spending quality time with the children and exploring God's wonderful world around us. One day we found a family of rock rabbits in the hills behind our house. Another day Mark arrived with a venomous puff adder (snake) he had killed with his bow and arrow. Our children never were bored for lack of things to do, for God provided them with all kinds of excitement through His creatures and the great outdoors!

We made friends with the European farmers and their families who lived in the area. One day Judy and Ben (not their real names) and their two children were visiting us. Judy and I were swinging our two little ones in our tire swings as I talked to her about Jesus. She asked me, "What do you mean when you talk about receiving Jesus and making a commitment to Him? I'm a church member, but I've never heard of this." I tried to explain, but she didn't understand.

Because of their love of hunting, Gene and Ben became great friends. They often had conversations about the Lord, and seeds were continually planted. We trusted God would use these to bear fruit. We showed gospel movies in the homes of some of the farmers. One of them was very convicted of his need for Jesus. Betty (not her real name), the wife, received Christ, but her husband concluded that salvation by grace through faith alone was too simple. Surely God would make him do something for his salvation. We explained that salvation is not cheap. The heavy price has already been paid by Jesus and is a gift to be received. Again we prayed that the Holy Spirit would bring him to simple saving faith.

The manager of Samba Ranch allowed us to conduct worship services on two of his farm compounds where no gospel witness was present. Since we spoke the Shona language, we freely entered this open door. Most Sundays, Gene drove into Triangle for worship services, and I took the children with me to local villages. Rebecca, our housekeeper who had worked for us since 1957 and was a wonderful Christian, went with us each week. She had moved from her home in Shabani to work in our home, as well as to help start new churches. I taught a Bible lesson to the adults while she taught the children. People were saved, lives were changed, and a church was begun because of God's working through us.

One day the tractor driver, Judge, who brought water in huge drums, had an accident on the farm tractor. God spared his life, and Gene witnessed to him. We learned that he had led a wicked life as a drunkard, thief, and brawler who had stabbed people. In fact, he had gone to court so many times and had stood before so many judges that he received the nickname, "Judge." God convicted this man of his sin, and he came to Christ in repentance and faith. His life was dramatically changed. He faithfully attended worship services, and Gene experienced the joy of baptizing "Judge" and his wife, along with others, in our round portable baptismal pool.

The new believers built a simple church building out of poles, mud, and thatch. In a pagan culture it stood as a tremendous witness to the power of God to change lives and bind them together into the body of Christ.

Because the nearest clinic was 25 miles away, sick people often came to us for help. We prayed for them and lovingly ministered to them in our limited way. I remember little Diana, who was blind because of measles. When her mother brought her to us, the girl's ears were badly infected. We did what we could and helped her get to the doctor in Triangle.

Weary travelers, sometimes almost dying of thirst from the blazing sun, passed near our house. We offered them cups of cold water in Jesus' name and told them about His love for them. Others had car trouble on the road not far from our house and approached us for help. We loaned them our pump or gave them patching material for flat tires, along with cool drinks or cups of hot tea and cookies. One man we assisted in this way later helped open a door for our witness in Triangle.

We also began services at a school on the outskirts of Triangle on the road to Samba Ranch. Our first Sunday there we noticed a 12-year-old boy enter the classroom. He was walking on his hands, dragging behind him like dead fish two shriveled legs with callused, knobby knees. He pulled himself up onto a seat and sat there in rapt attention as Gene preached the message of Jesus. His face was alive with interest and intelligence. His eyes reflected no bitterness at his condition, only wonder and joy at what he was experiencing as he heard of Jesus. He was present week after week, crawling through rain and mud, sunshine and dust to get there. After several weeks, Rwokuda Jachi accepted Jesus as his Savior and Lord. Later, he was baptized. Eventually he moved into Triangle and attended our main church there. He became a Sunday School teacher and youth leader. Because no high school existed in Triangle in those days, we helped

Rwokuda enroll in our Baptist High School across the country at Sanyati.

He didn't do well on his final exams, and his usually cheerful disposition was invaded by self-pity and frustration. Dejection, discouragement, and depression nearly dragged him under. But we prayed with him and encouraged him to take other courses and upgrade his high school studies by correspondence. Eventually he got a job as cashier in the Triangle butcher shop. While there, he shared with us his dream of going to the States to college. Each week he brought his paycheck to our house and handed it to Gene with these words, "One tenth belongs to God. Put the rest in the bank for my college education." Since he was living at home and his stepfather drank alcohol, he didn't want any of the money to go home with him.

When we saw how sincere he was about his desire to go to college, we started searching for scholarships for him. Eventually he was accepted at Gardner Webb College in North Carolina. He and our son Paul joined our daughter Beth there in 1980. Before he left, the European Christians at Triangle bought him a nice wheelchair. He received his bachelor of arts degree in 1984, took additional courses to enable him to repair electrical equipment, and returned to what was then called Zimbabwe, where he got a job teaching in a technical college. He was a great teacher, a tither of his income, and a deacon in his church. He married and had four children, two of whom are named for us.

In December, 1998, he brought some of his family to see us at Sanyati, where we were serving as volunteers after retirement. He told us he had diabetes and high blood pressure. Then in February 1999, while we were in Lesotho, he died and went to be with the Lord. How grateful we are for his wonderful witness through the years God gave him on earth and even in his death.

As we trusted God with all our hearts and quit trying to understand the why of everything, God gave us joy and used us to introduce His Son to those who otherwise might have never heard.

Chapter 5

Learning Patience

"Knowing that the testing of your faith produces patience. But let patience have its perfect work, that you may be perfect and complete, lacking nothing"

—James 1:3-4 (NKJV).

God still had much more to teach us.

While we lived at the farm, the Triangle Company provided a lot on which to build our house. Our Mission allowed Gene to first build the workers' quarters at the back of this lot. During the mornings, while the children were at school, Gene went to the lot and had his Quiet Time with the Lord. Then he worked with African builders to construct the two-room structure with a bath and small storeroom.

During 1965, after Rhodesia declared its independence from Britain, many countries showed their disapproval by refusing to trade with Rhodesia. Such sanctions caused a severe shortage of many items, especially gasoline. Consequently, by the end of December, the government introduced gasoline rationing. This meant we wouldn't have enough fuel to make the round trip to

Triangle each day. So on January 1, 1966, we moved into the still-unpainted workers' house Gene had been building. Since the place was so small, we built a pole and mud hut with thatched roof for Rebecca.

For our family of six, living in two rooms was definitely an adventure. It meant bringing only the barest of necessities with us and leaving the rest of our belongings at the farm. We extended the roof at the back of the house to make a large porch. Here we cooked, ate, washed, ironed, entertained, and lived for seven months. The burning afternoon sun streamed upon us, and the rain often drenched us. Mosquitoes, flies, and bugs were our constant companions. But we were gloriously happy. We rejoiced in God's provisions for us.

Soon Gene received the go-ahead to hire a contractor to begin construction of our house. It was exciting to be on site and watch it taking shape. We settled into the work of witnessing, making disciples among those around us, and starting new churches. We also made regular trips back to our growing church on the farm.

One Sunday, as Rebecca and I visited and invited people to Sunday School in one of the Triangle villages, we met Charlie Chitofu. He visited the service with us and sat with open mouth as we taught the Word. The next Sunday he attended again and mentioned that he was looking for work as a cook. I started praying both for his salvation and for him to find a job. About that time the contractor began work on our house. He lived in a trailer on our lot and needed a cook. Charlie became the contractor's cook. Before long, Charlie accepted Christ, was baptized, and began growing in the Lord. Later God called Charlie into the ministry, where he has served for many years.

Another Sunday, as we taught Sunday School under a tree in that same village, a man cutting sugar cane in the field nearby stopped his work and stepped up to the fence to listen. The next Sunday, instead of going to work, the man, Ephraim Maseko, attended church and while there accepted Christ as his personal Savior. Each week he refused to work on Sunday, saying he must go to church. Consequently, he was fired from his job. He found work on the adjoining Hippo Valley Sugar Estates and started worship services where he lived. He invited Gene to preach there. Ephraim

later found work in the new town of Chiredzi and began preaching
in that town. Eventually, he and his wife attended our Baptist
Seminary in Gwelo and then returned to be pastor of another new
church in our area. Later, they were appointed as home missionaries
under the Zimbabwe Baptist Convention, where they faithfully
served in planting and developing churches until his death in the
year 2000.

In July, 1966, we finally moved into our lovely new home. It
had been 11 months since we had returned from furlough. Rebecca
moved into the worker's quarters which we vacated. God had been
teaching us patience to wait for what He had promised.

Since I had often been concerned about how the Africans
viewed our higher living standards and nicer houses than they had, I
asked Rebecca one day, "Rebecca, would it be best if we lived on
par with the average African? Would we have a better witness that
way?"

Rebecca looked at me with her sweet smile and piercing eyes
and said with conviction in her voice, "Oh, no, Madam. You didn't
come to pull us down but to pull us up and show us a better way,
not only through the gospel but also in your lifestyle. You can share
with us what you have."

I thought about this and prayed about it through the years. At
our appointment service, Dr. Baker James Cauthen had told us, "As
you go, take your possessions in your hands and not in your hearts."
I continually prayed that I would never allow the possessions with
which God had blessed us to be in my heart where I would cling to
them. I never wanted my joy to be in what I had but in Him alone.

I also learned it's not what we have, but rather what we do with
what we have that really counts. I found out I could share cold
water from my refrigerator and ice from my freezer in a glass of
fruit drink with the African who had no refrigerator or freezer. We
could offer rides in our vehicle to those who had no car. We could
help the needy and give out Christ's love each day.

At this time, colonialism and segregation both thrived in
Rhodesia. The color of our skin dictated where and, to some extent,
how we lived. The company had set aside land for our mission
house in the European village. It was among the European staff
houses. Later, in the late 1970s the company began hiring African

staff, so we eventually had African neighbors, too.

All the houses in our village had beautiful lawns and lush flower and vegetable gardens. Since the company included us among those who received unlimited free water, I had no excuse not to have a nice yard. So I then faced the great challenge of landscaping our garden, which was then raw bush.

I didn't have a clue how to go about this, and Gene wasn't particularly interested or knowledgeable in this area. So I bought a good book on gardening in Rhodesia, joined the local garden club, and went to work, with the help of our gardener. Since our neighbors examined every aspect of these "non-conformist" American missionaries, I also prayed a lot. I wanted our garden to be a witness for God.

Plants were relatively cheap at our local nursery, so soon our yard was blooming and glowing with color and beauty. We also planted vegetables and fruit trees. This proved to be the way I met many of my neighbors. Often people driving by stopped and congratulated me on what had been accomplished in the yard. Some of these people later professed Christ as Savior.

The garden was also a way to witness to young men who needed work. During school holidays, I hired several students from our church to work in the garden. One was Roy Njini. Today Roy is director of Theological Education by Extension at the Baptist Seminary in Gweru (Gwelo). Another was Lot Chitogwa who today is a faithful Christian high school teacher and married to the treasurer of the Zimbabwe Baptist Seminary. I asked the Lord to send me a very special worker whom I could disciple. One day at the beginning of the holidays, I heard a knock on our door. I opened it to find a young man who said, "Please, Madam, I need a job so I can get money for school fees."

"I'm sorry," I answered, "I don't need any more workers. I've already hired enough for the holidays."

But the young man persisted. "I'll do anything. Please don't turn me away," he begged. "My father is dead, and I sold my clothes to get money for first term. Now I don't have any more clothes to sell and no money to pay for second term."

We heard this kind of plea all the time and had to harden ourselves a bit to all the needs with which we were confronted. But now the Lord reminded me of my request for someone to disciple. "Lord, could this young man be the answer to my prayer?"

So I said to the young man, whose name was Alex Moyo, "Return here tomorrow, and you can work for a few days."

When he arrived the next day, I purposely gave him a hard task to accomplish—digging out a dead tree, roots, and all. This job would have taken most gardeners a week to finish. Alex finished the work in one day. That day, as I participated in Bible study with the workers, Alex was very interested and seemed hungry to learn. At the end of the day, I talked with him further and asked him about his relationship with the Lord. He said he was a believer but a member of another church.

He came back the next day, and the next, and the next. I continued to be impressed with his hard work, dependability, and honesty. He started attending our church with the other young men who worked for us and who enthusiastically participated in a discipleship study. Studying God's Word, he realized he had never been born again, and he accepted Jesus as his Lord and Savior. Then he started discipling others.

Alex stayed with us many years, even moving with us to our next place of ministry. He grew in his understanding of God as a loving Father who delighted in supplying his needs. He learned to forgive an older brother who had wronged him. Eventually he trained as a nurse, which is his calling today.

We lived on the corner of two dirt roads. One was the main thoroughfare for hilos—huge tractors with long trailers which transport sugar cane to the sugar mill. Vehicles which looked something like road sweepers spread a type of molasses, a byproduct of the sugar industry, on the main road to cut down the dust. But when it rained, the molasses was washed off, and we felt like we were drowning in dust again. By the early 1980s, plans were developing to pave the road. When they eventually started paving the road, the construction kept my garden continually messed up.

With tongue in cheek, I wrote the following poem to our good friend in charge of the roads. I also sent him the other two poems that tell what God was teaching me through all this.

DUST

*Did you ever eat a dust sandwich? Did you ever drink some
dust tea?*
*Did you ever wake in the morning, to find dust had settled on
thee?*

*Did you ever walk in your garden and find dust on each leaf
and flow'r?*
*Did you ever scrub house and clean it, yet see dust collecting
that hour?*

*Did you ever take a breath and discover your lungs had become
two dust bags?*
*Did you ever look in your closet to see dust on your clothes just
like rags?*

*If you've never had these adventures, I invite you to 9 Milne
Street.*
*Just stay here a day, and I'm certain Mtilikwe Drive will be
paved nice and neat.*

LESSONS FROM A GARDEN

I'm grateful to Triangle for good things galore,
For water abundant, firewood left at our door;
For good, rich manure, for medical care,
For being the means through which God answers prayer.

I asked God for patience, to take things in stride.
He sent me to Triangle where I could abide.
I'd work in my garden and get it just right,
Then here came a bulldozer from morn until night.

When I'd start to complain, I'd hear my Lord say,
"I'm answering your prayer, Child, in my kind of way.
So look at your garden and start it again,
I'll give you new ideas, a new kind of plan."

So, Triangle, I love you! Please do take my word,
You've taught me some lessons that are not absurd.
I want to keep learning, but give me a break:
Please finish the roadway without a mistake!

WHAT WILL I DO WITH DUST?

I don't like dust!
Red dust, white fine powdery dust,
I detest it all!

But it's here, and I am too.
It gets on my clothes, it clogs up my nose,
My whole house reeks of this thing.
I don't know how to keep it all clean.
My garden cries out in despair
For this dust it always must wear.
Oh, what am I going to do?

I can't get rid of the dust,
Though I once hoped it might be.
So I'll have to learn to live with it,
And thank God for it,
And ask Him to turn the dust into gold,
And use it as a mold
To form His likeness in me.

The garden wasn't the only means through which God taught me patience. In June, 1972, the back problem I had experienced since 1965 degenerated into a dreadfully painful ruptured disc. After various tests and treatments, the doctor told me I must have surgery immediately or risk permanent damage to the nerves in my right leg.

Paul was in school in Triangle; John and Beth were in Gwelo 210 miles away; Mark was preparing to leave for his first year of college in the States. This didn't seem like the ideal time for me to be 300 miles away in Salisbury, having a surgery that would require a lengthy recuperation. While Gene, our Christian friends, and I prayed for my healing, God assured us that surgery was a part of His plan.

The surgeon removed my lower two lumbar discs and insisted that I lie flat on my back for a week. When he released me from the hospital, he advised me to speed up my recovery by swimming every day. Not knowing how to swim, I ignored his advice and continued to experience pain and weakness. This situation led me to become impatient and discouraged again.

Finally, the whole family encouraged me to learn to swim. We were allowed to use Triangle's lovely pool. So putting aside my pride and wearing a child's water wings, I began my swimming lessons. Gene patiently worked with me until I could stay afloat and finally could swim. Sure enough, the swimming worked wonders on my back. Soon it was strong again and felt better than it had in months. Again, God had taught me patience as I trusted Him and obeyed His servant's expert advice.

Chapter 6

Living Through a Civil War

"God is our refuge and strength, an ever-present help in trouble. Therefore we will not fear . . . "
—Psalm 46:1-2.

"He who dwells in the shelter of the Most High will rest in the shadow of the Almighty"
—Psalm 91:1.

After we moved to the Triangle Estates, the political unrest that had begun to boil in the early 1960s continued to grow. The newly formed black political parties advocated revolution. Two of these rival groups were the Zimbabwe African National Union-Patriotic Front (ZANU-PF), led by Robert Mugabe of the Shona tribe, and the Zimbabwe African People's Union (ZAPU), led by Joshua Nkomo of the Ndebele tribe. With headquarters outside the country, they led many of the youth, both male and female, out of the country to be trained in communist guerrilla warfare. Some went to Marxist Mozambique or Angola; others went to Zambia or Botswana. Rural teenagers were enticed, and sometimes conscripted, to leave their homes and join the movement. Some of the most educated ended up in East Germany or Cuba. After their training, they began to infiltrate the country with weapons.

Triangle, in the southeastern part of Rhodesia, was just over 50 miles from the border with Mozambique. The guerrillas, often referred to by the Africans as "vakomana"[1], entered our part of the country by following the Lundi River that flowed through the Triangle Estates. Although they moved through the area during the war, only one incident occurred in which they killed someone on the Estates. Heading into the tribal trust lands west of us, they mingled among the Africans in rural farm villages and spread their propaganda. Each night they gathered the villagers and indoctrinated them. They taught them revolution songs and chanted, "Pasi naJesu! Pamberi neChimurenga!" ("Down with Jesus. Up with the Revolution!") They taught the villagers to destroy schools, churches, hospitals, and stores.

From the beginning, they instigated riots in the cities and spread hatred toward whites. They also set off bombs in downtown department stores and planted land mines on gravel roads and main highways.

Prime Minister Ian Smith began to build up the Rhodesian army by drafting all able-bodied white males. Many Rhodesian blacks also joined the country's security forces. Numerous men from other countries joined as mercenaries also.

If any of the African villagers had a son or daughter in the country's security forces or if they appeared pro-government, they were called "sell-outs" and were often tortured or killed. Young boys and girls in the villages all over the country were used as *mijiba* (Shona for informers or spies) to run errands for the guerrillas and spy on their families and neighbors. They were sent each night to find out where the security forces were. Then, at 4 the next morning, after taking food from villagers, they cooked for the guerrillas.

Alex, the young man who had come to me pleading for work, had been a *mujiba* (singular for *mijiba*) before he worked for us. One day when he was 16, he was forced to take food to a group of guerrillas. The Rhodesian army attacked the group while they were eating. Though many died in the fighting, Alex survived. He was captured by government soldiers and taken for interrogation.

His interrogators used psychological tactics to persuade Alex to give them information. They put him in a dark room where a "ghost" appeared to him. The "ghost" said, "I am the ghost of a mujiba who was captured and put in this very room. They told me that a snake would be put in here and it would bite me. If I told them the truth, I would not die from the bite. If I lied, I would die. I lied to them, was bitten, and died. And you will lie, then die, and join me as a ghost. Ha! Ha! Ha!"

Alex was not troubled by the "ghost" because he could see it was a man under a white sheet. But when they put a snake in the room and he was bitten, his fear of death caused him to give them the information they were seeking. Alex was sentenced to eight months in jail. After his release, afraid to go back to his village, he arrived at Triangle to stay with his brother. That was when the Lord brought him to our house and eventually to Christ.

Our personal realization of how serious the conflict was becoming came one weekend in the mid-1970s when we visited one of our rural churches. Our custom was to set up our sleeping tent at a school, where we would conduct worship services and show a film on the life of Christ. As we pulled up that day, however, the church leaders met our car and said, "You had better come and sleep in our village tonight."

We did as they suggested and went ahead with the meetings, but we noticed that everyone was very tense. The next day, as we got ready to leave, the leaders asked us not to come back until they notified us it was safe. They told us that because guerrillas were nearby, we were putting our lives, as well as theirs, in danger by simply being there.

For several years, we had little contact with these dear rural people. One leader visited Triangle several times to get Bibles, tracts, and Sunday School literature. Then he began to slack off in this effort because the guerrillas were confiscating Bibles and Christian books. A Catholic priest living at a mission station in the area was murdered by the guerrillas.

Influenced by godless communism, many guerrillas warned the people not to read or even possess a Bible or other Christian literature. The women were warned not to wear their church uniforms. Some who defied the warnings had their uniforms torn from their bodies. In certain areas, Africans were not allowed to meet together for worship. They were told that Christianity is the white man's religion. They were told they must return to the worship of ancestral spirits. They were told they could worship Mwari (God) but not Jesus Christ. Many who disobeyed this order were severely beaten or even killed. In certain areas of the country, the church went underground.

We curtailed a lot of our night meetings in the outlying area of Triangle, on the adjoining Hippo Valley Sugar Estates, and in the government-seat town of Chiredzi. Even when traveling in the daytime, we learned to be suspicious of any disturbance in the road that could possibly be a land mine.

During this time, our children were in boarding school in Gwelo, 210 miles away. We formed car pools with other parents whose children also attended school in Gwelo. On one of these trips, when Gene was travelling with Beth and Paul, along with four other children, they missed an ambush by two hours. They had passed the 50-kilometer peg at 2 p.m. Two hours later, the vakomana stopped a bus at this spot. A European man, his wife, and 12-year-old son came upon the scene and were fired on. Though the boy was hit in the arm, and their car riddled with bullets, they managed to escape. Such incidents repeated themselves many times during the war, prompting us to remember that God is our refuge and strength.

Because of the many ambushes on the highways in the Southeastern section of the country and even to Gwelo, the government provided military-escorted convoys in which to travel. One convoy left Triangle at 6 a.m. and the other at noon. We traveled with this convoy 50 miles to Ngundu Halt, where we connected with other vehicles going north to Fort Victoria. If we were going toward South Africa, we met another southbound convoy. If we were going to Gwelo, we joined another convoy at Fort Victoria for the rest of the journey. We traveled this way for several years.

A military vehicle was at the front and another at the rear of the convoy. Soldiers on each military vehicle carried sub-machine guns, and most private vehicles in the convoy had weapons sticking out their windows. In doing this, they looked like porcupines. Gene and I decided not to carry a gun. We took advantage of the convoys, but since this wasn't our war, we tried to maintain our neutrality. As visitors in the country, we were there to preach Jesus to everyone, not to engage in partisan conflict.

In spite of all the weapons on the convoys, sometimes they were hit by gunfire. One time I was supposed to take some women to a Woman's Missionary Union (WMU) convention in Gwelo. Our truck had been in the shop for repairs and wasn't ready until about 9 a.m. the day I was to leave. I needed to be in Fort Victoria by noon to meet the last convoy of the day going to Gwelo. If I waited for the noon convoy from Triangle, I would have to travel alone in the late afternoon, when attacks were usually more likely. So after Gene, the African women, and I prayed for God's direction, we decided that we should travel the first part of the journey without the convoy. God protected us, and we arrived safely. Later, however, we learned that the 6 a.m. convoy I had intended to take had been attacked. God used car trouble to protect us from this danger!

All of us missionaries had the option of transferring to another field during this time of war. Gene and I prayed much about whether to take this option, but we felt God was leading us to stay. Though we couldn't travel as freely, we found open doors and open hearts all around us. From the beginning, we had a fruitful ministry among the Africans, but it was much slower among the Europeans. The Europeans respected us, but when we tried to talk to them about the Lord, they would usually answer, "Religion is a very private matter. That's a topic we won't discuss." So Gene and I decided to continue to love them and, together with a handful of other believers, pray for their salvation.

One of the first ministries we began after moving to Triangle was that of teaching Scripture in the schools, both black and white. In Rhodesia every denomination had the freedom to teach students the Bible from its perspective. This was called "Right of Entry." In the beginning, we didn't have many Baptists. Our own children attended the small European school through 7th grade and were in our class. But since there were no other ministers or missionaries besides Catholics in those days, we were allowed to teach all Protestants who wanted to attend. Soon the Protestant parents requested that we teach their children. We gladly went through this open door. This gave us good contacts, not only with the children, but also with their parents.

My mother visited us a few months before furlough in 1969 and helped teach our Scripture classes. What joy to have her minister alongside us for those months!

When He revived my heart a few years earlier, God also gave me a greater love for the Europeans. While in Shabani, I had resented many Europeans because of the way they treated the Africans. However, we did have a small ministry among them, and a few were our very dear friends and remain so to this day. God was teaching me that He loved the sinful, prejudiced Europeans as much as He loved the sinful, prejudiced Africans. He wanted all to be saved. Our primary mission work was among the Africans, but we were to be His witnesses to all we met.

We held our main African worship meetings on Sunday mornings and afternoons, so Gene began an English-speaking worship service in the European school auditorium on Sunday evenings for the Europeans. It was like what we had done earlier in Shabani. At first, only a handful attended. But in 1971, this began to change. God transferred to Triangle a wonderful Baptist couple. Peter Rees, a deacon and our new bank manager, and his wife Joan were a blessing to us in every way! At the same time, the Lord sent John Morrison-Young as the new headmaster of our children's school. John was a strong believer of Brethren background, and his wife Trish was an evangelical Anglican. A dear Pentecostal couple, Eddie and Elizabeth Jacques, already lived in Triangle.

In November, 1972, God led us four women to begin a meeting for ladies. Each of us led the Bible study once a month. We invited our neighbors and friends to our homes each week. By January, 1973, two of the women had committed their lives to Jesus. One of these was our next-door neighbor who had delved in spiritualism, drugs, and immorality. She had been full of skepticism and unbelief. But as she studied the Bible, God convicted her and gave her new life.

New women continued to attend. By February, we had doubled our original number. A few months later we had tripled it. Most of these women were from mainline denominational backgrounds but had never before understood what it meant to receive Jesus by faith. One day a newcomer to the group asked a new believer what it meant to her to be a Christian. Selma thought a minute and said, "Well, it's like this. I used to hear of people who were told to either deny Jesus or die. I would think, 'Oh, you fool, why don't you deny Him and save your life. Then afterwards you can tell God you really didn't mean it.' Now I understand why they couldn't deny Him. I couldn't either now, for He is my life, my all, and I would gladly die for Him."

As the women accepted Christ, their attitude toward the Africans changed. They developed a kindness and patience with them and began to see them as their neighbors. They began giving their maids and garden workers time off to attend church. (Several of their employees accepted Jesus and joined our church.)

Their husbands took notice of the changes in their wives' lives. When the husbands went on "call-up" duty in the army and faced death, they developed a greater sensitivity toward spiritual matters. A number of them also accepted Christ, so Gene and I led Bible studies in their homes to help them grow in the Lord. Many of these new believers started attending our Sunday-night worship services.

In 1976, God sent us a wonderful young man who was a part of the Southern Baptist Journeyman program. That program sends recent college graduates to the overseas mission field for two years. His name was Tim Cearley, and he came to work with our youth, both African and European. This young man was willing to take the risk of working in a country at war in order to do God's will, and for that God greatly blessed his ministry. After Tim completed his two years with us, he went to Southwestern Baptist Theological Seminary in Fort Worth, Texas, where he met his precious wife Charlotte. Together, they returned to Zimbabwe as church developers. After 10 years in that ministry, they transferred to Mozambique, where they presently work.

While Tim was with us, one of the 11-year-old girls, who attended the Sunday School he led and was in the Scripture class Trish taught, died of cerebral malaria. Gene was acquainted with her father through Lion's Club, and I knew her mother through garden club. Since they had no church affiliation, they asked Gene to conduct the memorial service. As a direct result of her death, her parents, older brother, and later, her older sister professed Jesus as Savior and became powerful witnesses for Him.

In spite of all the victories God was giving, we often experienced discouragement. The situation in which we lived was very tense. With war on all sides of us, a large air force base was set up at the airport about 12 miles from Triangle. Race relations were not good, and Africans were often suspicious of us because we were white.

In February, 1977, the African pastor of our Runyararo Baptist Church was arrested and served four-and-one-half months in jail for failing to report the presence of terrorists at a meeting he had attended. The situation in the country was very difficult for the Africans. Regardless of what they did, they seemed to find themselves in trouble. If the pastor had reported the guerrillas' presence, he would have been called a "sell-out" and would have been in still greater trouble with other blacks than with the government.

As the war continued to escalate, the government called for national days of prayer and fasting. Prayer meetings were begun at 5 a.m. each Sunday. In October, 1977, God led us to have a multiracial, interdenominational crusade in the European school hall. Though the services were entirely in English, almost a third of the audience was black.

In spite of the danger of traveling after dark, many people journeyed 20 miles or more to attend. Night after night—in a land where racial tensions abounded and where war was causing so much hatred and death—the races and denominations united in love and prayer. They blended their voices as a choir and sang praises to our Lord. Our evangelist, Rev. John Broom, pastor of the European Gwelo Baptist Church, brought stirring messages from God's Word. Both black and white believers gave thrilling testimonies of what God had done in their lives.

Seeing the salvation of many Europeans for whom we had prayed for many years brought great joy! One of these was our doctor—a compassionate, religious man. One night when the invitation was given, he prayed to receive Jesus and then stepped out to make his decision public. He later testified that years before, when he had been confirmed in his church, he had not understood what receiving Jesus meant. Another friend from another church who, with her husband, sang in the choir, later testified, "At first I just came to sing in the choir. But then I found something here I needed, and now I truly belong to Jesus. This has been the most wonderful week of my life." Her husband agreed.

By the time Tim left in 1978, the war had greatly intensified, especially in the rural areas. Missionaries often were targets for hatred and murder. On June 15, 1978, the war tragically touched our group of missionaries. Our dear friend and co-worker, Archie Dunaway, was stabbed to death by a band of guerrillas who entered the Sanyati Baptist Mission Station. In 1971 Archie and his wife Margaret had transferred to Rhodesia from Nigeria. He was mainte-nance supervisor at the Sanyati Baptist Hospital and area evangelist. Margaret was a nurse at the hospital and directed a school for mid-wives.

Archie and Margaret had an agreement that the first to arrive home after their work was finished in the evening would leave a note if he or she went to visit another house. That evening of June 15 when Archie came home, his wife was not there, nor was there a note. He decided to go to the hospital to walk his wife home. As he entered the hospital, he came upon a group of four guerrillas indoc-trinating the African staff with their propaganda. They grabbed Archie, took him outside, and brutally murdered him.

In the meantime Margaret completed her delivery of a baby, left the hospital by another door, and returned home where she didn't find Archie or a note from him. Phoning the other missionaries and realizing no one had seen him, she became concerned that perhaps he was sick somewhere on the mission compound. To search for him they began driving the roads and carrying flashlights as they walked the paths to search for him.

With all this activity and lights from the cars and flashlights, the guerrillas must have assumed that the security forces had arrived and were looking for them. So they fled. Consequently, we believe that the death of Archie saved the lives of all the other missionaries there. About 13 hours after he was killed, his body was finally located outside the hospital.

The memorial service for Archie was held at the Gwelo Baptist Church, which was packed with Africans as well as with missionar-ies and other Europeans. Feeling the weight of the atrocity commit-ted by one of his people, an African pastor prayed with broken heart, "O God, forgive us. Forgive us for this terrible thing."

Missionary Mary Monroe sang one of Archie's favorite songs, "Follow Me" by Ira F. Stanphill. Hardly a dry eye existed among us as she sang the last verse,

> *"Oh Jesus, if I die upon a foreign field some day,*
> *'Twould be no more than love demands; No less could I repay;*
> *No greater love hath mortal man than for a friend to die'*
> *These are the words He gently spoke to me:*
> *'If just a cup of water I place within your hand,*
> *Then just a cup of water Is all that I demand;'*
> *But if by death to living They can Thy glory see,*
> *I'll take my cross and follow close to Thee."*[2]

The missionary who preached at the funeral spoke of Archie's victory over death. He then said to those who killed him, "We forgive you and want you to come to Jesus so He can forgive and cleanse you of this terrible sin." As the service closed by the congregation's singing "To God Be The Glory," we were assured that God was glorified in Archie's death as well as in his life.

Nine days after Archie was killed at Sanyati in the northwestern part of the country, eight Pentecostal missionaries and four children were bludgeoned to death on their mission station in the eastern highlands. I was at home alone that evening when the news came over the radio telling of this tragedy. Our three oldest children were in the States; Paul was in school in Gwelo; and Gene was away at meetings. I sobbed as the brutality of those murders was vividly described. For the first time since the war began, I was terribly afraid. I cried out, "Oh Lord, how much longer are you going to allow this to go on? How many more of your children are going to have to die? Will Gene and I be next?"

The next day I went down by a quiet stream to pray. I told the Lord, "Father, I can't stay here with this kind of fear in my heart. I don't want to leave unless you're calling us to go. But you're going to have to give me peace if we stay. Show us what to do. I put our lives and our future in your hands."

God began to remind me again of the words in 2 Timothy 1:7 that He didn't give me the spirit of fear. He reminded me of the words in 1 John 4:18 that perfect love drives out fear. He also reminded me of Mordecai's words to Queen Esther, " . . . 'Yet who knows whether you have come to the kingdom for such a time as this?' " Esther 4:14 (NKJV). I knew He wanted us to stay. By the time Gene returned home, my heart was at peace. We talked and prayed together, and peace descended on both of us. It was the peace of being in the center of God's will. God didn't tell us that nothing bad would happen to us if we stayed. Except for furlough times, we remained throughout the whole war, and God's peace sustained us.

Hundreds of mission stations, including ours at Sasame in Gokwe, had to close. All our missionary personnel were evacuated from Sanyati to other parts of the country, but African staff kept the hospital and school operating. Drs. Maurice Randall and John Monroe made periodic trips to Sanyati to minister to the sick and encourage the staff.

This war was not only nationalistic and political in nature,but it was also a spiritual battle in which Satan fought against the church of Jesus Christ. Against their wills, many of the freedom fighters were trained as guerrillas. Some were abducted as youngsters from schools, including mission schools. Some had, as children, received Christ but became hardened through their indoctrination and exposure to violence and terror. When they found Christians who were willing to die rather than deny Christ, many of them were convicted and strengthened in what they had been taught as children. Numbers of these did not commit the atrocities against the Christians. In fact, some attended services, read the Bible, and even took Bibles to the villagers.

During 1978, two moderate black nationalist leaders, Bishop Abel Muzorewa of the African National Congress and Ndabaningi Sithole of the Zimbabwe African National Union-NDONGA (ZANU-NDONGA), signed an agreement with Ian Smith to distribute the governing of the country among the three of them. For a short period of time, the country's name was changed to Zimbabwe-Rhodesia. This arrangement was unacceptable to other nationalist leaders and other African nations and it was never recognized by Western governments.

Finally in 1979, Smith, Muzorewa, Robert Mugabe, and Joshua Nkomo, along with others, went to London to sit around the conference tables with Margaret Thatcher and the British and work out a new constitution which would be acceptable to all. A cease-fire was declared for December 31, after more than 12 years of civil war.[3] Elections were held in 1980, and Robert Mugabe became the new prime minister (later called president) in a landslide victory. On April 17, 1980, the country gained its independence from Britain. It became known as Zimbabwe, meaning houses of stone (from two Shona words, *dzimba dzamabge*).

The war had taken a heavy toll upon the people and the land. More than 20,000 civilians of all races were killed, along with thousands of guerrillas and security-force members comprising all races. Approximately 45 missionaries of various denominations were also killed. Many years would be required to recover from the physical and emotional effects of the war and to build up trust among the peoples. Tensions existed not only among blacks and whites but also among the rival African political parties, especially between the Ndebele and Shona tribes. Some tribes did not want to accept the elected government, and dissidents kept trying to cause disturbances and gain control for Joshua Nkomo and the Ndebele. Mugabe wisely decided to share power with Nkomo, by making him vice-president, and by bringing into the nation a policy of reconciliation.

Soon after the war ended, a Zimbabwe Baptist youth conference was held at the Baptist camp in Gweru, the new name for Gwelo. Here a call for reconciliation among Christians occurred. Many of those present had been on opposing sides of the conflict and needed to forgive each other. The speaker, using Christ as our example, poured out his heart with a message of love, forgiveness, and reconciliation. In his invitation, he appealed to those who needed to make things right with another who was present to go to him or her and do so.

I was singing and praying when a young African girl came to me and said, "Please forgive me." Not recognizing her and trying to decide who she was and where I had known her, I looked into her eyes and wondered for what I was to forgive her. At the same time, I embraced her and said, "Of course I forgive you." Standing there with our arms around each other and with healing tears flowing, I realized that she most likely had been a guerrilla who had participated in the killing of missionaries and other whites. She couldn't go to them, but she let me represent them as God dealt with her about the enormity of her sin. I praise God that He used me to help bring His forgiveness and reconciliation into her life.

Though the physical war was over, a great spiritual battle was still going on for the souls of people in our land, and much more healing would need to take place. We're glad God led us on a journey that allowed us to be a part of that healing.

[1]A Shona word for "boys", even though girls were also guerrillas.
[2]©1953 Singspiration Music (admin by Brentwood-Benson Music Publishing, Inc.) All Rights Reserved. Used by permission.
[3]No official date is given as to when the war actually began. It became more noticeable in 1972.

Chapter 7

Waiting on the Lord

"Rest in the Lord, and wait patiently for him; Do not fret . . ."
—Psalm 37:7 (NKJV).

"But those who wait on the Lord Shall renew their strength; . . ."
—Isaiah 40:31 (NKJV).

"The Lord is good to those who wait for Him, To the soul who seeks Him"
—Lamentations 3:25 (NKJV).

After basking in the beauty of the Triangle Estates, rejoicing in God's protection throughout the war, loving and ministering to the wonderful people, and enjoying every minute of seeing all the neat things God did in their lives and in the churches, God gave us a new call. That call came in 1982, but we didn't move until 1984, more than 18 years after we had arrived in Triangle.

This time God called us across the country to the raw bush of rural Gokwe, a vast tribal trust land where the Africans were subsistence farmers. They eked out a living on their seven to 10 acres of land, growing maize, rupoko, and cotton in depleted sandy soil. Most supplemented these main crops with pumpkins, watermelons, sorghum, and other grains, while some added peanuts, sunflowers, okra, and beans. They used stubborn oxen to plow their ground. An adult was usually behind the plow, while a child walked beside the oxen to keep them on track.

Most families owned a few cattle, donkeys, chickens, some dogs, and a large herd of goats. A few raised ducks or sheep. Driving through the area, one had to share the roads with these creatures. A local fable about that situation goes like this:

"One day a donkey, goat and dog were passengers in a taxi. The fare was $5.00. At their stop, the donkey gave the driver a $10.00 bill, got out, and stood on the road waiting for his change. The dog gave the driver the correct amount, and as he was jumping out of the taxi, the goat slipped by him and ran away without paying. Not to be outdone by all this, the driver sped away, keeping the donkey's change. That's why today goats are always on the run across the road in front of cars. Donkeys, waiting on their change, stubbornly stand in the middle of the road. And dogs, trying to help the donkey get his change, habitually chase cars."

No lush green fields of irrigated sugar cane existed in this area, because no water was available for irrigation. In most years, a low rainfall level made farming a great risk. But during the years of good rainfall, the populace reaped a plentiful harvest and were a happy people. Their cash crop of cotton brought in extra money for luxuries such as bicycles, furniture, radios, battery-powered TVs, and cement-block houses with tin roofs to replace their mud huts with thatched roofs.

Most in our area were of the Shona tribe, whose language we spoke. Many Tongas and a sprinkling of Ndebeles, whose languages we didn't speak, also lived in our area.

During the war, in 1976, the Sasame Mission Station in Gokwe had to close. After the missionaries, clinic workers, and national pastors left, guerrillas forced the people to destroy the mission's buildings as well as church buildings and clinics in the area. No one will ever know how much the local people suffered because of the war! They had no schools, no clinics, no churches, few stores, and their fields and households were frequently raided by the guerrillas. Security forces brought their own brand of terror and trials to the people. Buses didn't run for at least four years, so during that time the only means of transportation the majority of the people had was by foot or bicycle.

In 1982 when the Zimbabwe Baptist Mission voted to rebuild the station and Gokwe clinics, they asked us to move there and focus on evangelism and church development. God had already been turning our hearts toward rural work, so we were ready to accept this new assignment. Gene was also elected coordinator of the People Who Care Project. This was a partnership venture with Louisiana Baptists. Through it, buildings were to be rebuilt, wells were to be drilled, food was to be distributed, and evangelism was to be done. Fellow missionaries Dr. Rob and Eloise Garrett were also involved in this project. They worked out of the Sanyati Mission Station 60 miles away but planned to move to Sasame when it was rebuilt.

In order to get to the Sasame Mission, we had to cross several rivers. Coming from Sanyati, the washboard gravel road passed through villages, fields, and settlements and into a barren stretch which looked like someone had poured salt on the land to lay it waste. Then the lonely dirt road narrowed as it wound through wooded hills. It crossed the wide, bridgeless Sasame River that was dry most of the year. Just past the river, we could take a shortcut down a bush trail, passing through heavily populated villages, crossing the Tare River—again with no bridge—and onto the mission station. A longer route took us across the Tare River on a narrow low-level bridge. On that route, we would pass many picturesque baobab trees.

Many hazards existed on the road to Sanyati. One of the worst was getting stuck behind a huge truck carrying cotton bales to the gin. In the dry season, the dust was thick, and it was impossible to see far enough ahead to pass safely. Dust was a fact of life throughout Gokwe. Wherever we went it, seemed to follow us. Sometimes in October or November before the rains began, strong winds stirred up dust from different types of soils in such a way that the horizon ahead of us often took on an eerie glow of multiple colors.

Traveling from Gweru or other places south, we turned off at

Kwe Kwe onto a paved road that led to the government-seat town of Gokwe.[1] Coming from Harare or other places north, we left the main highway just south of Kadoma and traveled an hour or more on a one-lane paved road until it joined the road from Kwe Kwe to Gokwe. Meeting another car on this narrow road was truly an adventure. Each driver would pull over to his side of the road with one wheel on the pavement and the other on the gravel, then continue without any loss of time. From Gokwe, we took the rough dirt road down the escarpment, around frightening curves, across the Svisvi River, again with no bridge. Arriving home, the 120-mile trip from Kwe Kwe usually took three hours.

In the early years during the rainy season, we often were stranded for a few hours because the rivers would rise, and we couldn't cross until they went down. Once the water receded, to get across the wet sand we had to put our Toyota into 4-wheel drive and push the accelerator to the floorboard. On some of the black clay roads, even our four-wheel-drive vehicle sometimes became stuck in mud that held us like a vise.

When we moved to Sasame, the government was in the process of paving the road from Kwe Kwe to Gokwe. In later years, the road was paved from Gokwe down the escarpment, past the mission station, and northward. High-level bridges were built over all the rivers. This change was a blessing to our welfare and to the Lord's work, but once again we had to wait patiently for this to happen.

Once Gene and I made the decision to move to Sasame, I was ready to go. But as usual we were slowed by many hindrances. One delay was caused by our son John's illness, which I will describe more fully in chapter 9. Another was Rob Garrett's illness and then his return to the States for by-pass surgery.

Delays also occurred in the building of our house, which was being constructed by Stateside volunteers and local nationals. Communication with those building the house was difficult since no phone was available. We could telephone Sanyati and ask the people there to get radio messages to Sasame. But we didn't always receive an answer.

Impatient to get moved, and hearing that the building was progressing well, in January, 1984 we scheduled a moving van for the end of February. A week before we were to move, we received word that the volunteers building the house were having difficulty obtaining windowpanes. Gene put them in touch with a company where the panes were available and reminded them of our moving date.

Hearing no further word from them, we began our move on our scheduled date. All our furniture went in the moving van. Since we would arrive the day before the moving van was scheduled to arrive, we took camping gear and some food with us in our pick-up. After spending the night with friends, Gene and I, along with our son, John, our gardener, Alex, our dog, Rex, and a very frightened caged cat, set out the next morning. Alex and John rode with the animals in the back of the pick-up. We all remember vividly how the cat meowed almost the whole nine hours of the trip in spite of having been given tranquilizers.

When we pulled into the mission station at sunset, no one was there to greet us. We drove to our house and found it far from finished. We wondered, "What to do now?" No hotels were around, we had no friends with which to stay—nothing, except the unfinished house. Gene located some of the Stateside volunteers who were building the house. They apologized profusely. After the volunteers said they didn't realize we were moving now, we all determined that somehow communications had broken down.

That night I fixed us some camp-style supper. Exhausted from the trip, we threw our sleeping bags down in the midst of the building rubble. We believed we could camp out indefinitely. But what would we do with our furniture when it arrived the next morning? Too tired to try and figure it out, we committed our problem to the Lord and went to sleep.

Early the next morning the construction crew showed Gene an almost-completed, two-room storehouse on our lot where they had been keeping building materials. The workers rounded up helpers and moved the materials elsewhere; then we hastily cleaned that storage facility. We decided that Gene and I would live in one room and store our furniture in the other. We also found two rooms in the main house that were nearing completion, so we prepared these for John and Alex. Just as we completed our preparations, the moving van arrived with our furniture.

I closely monitored the movers and directed the placing of each item that came from the van. Because our new home was in the bush three hours from town, I had brought quite a bit of food. "This must not end up in the storeroom with the furniture," I kept telling everyone. I was glad I had labeled the boxes! Despite my best efforts, some needed items ended up on the bottom of a stack of boxes and had to be dug out later.

We also created a makeshift, lean-to kitchen at the side of the storeroom. We lived this way for the next three months. Gene and John worked alongside the volunteers and nationals in completing our house. In spite of some of the inconveniences, we knew we were right where God wanted us and on His schedule.

Meanwhile, a devastating drought in the area caused terrible hunger. As a result, our mission developed a program called Food for Work. In order to feed as many people as possible, the large crew of African laborers changed each Monday. Since each work day began with an evangelistic service, many people heard the gospel as a result of this building project as well as a result of the two other mission residences that were built later.

While they built our house, we also worked with the volunteers to do other ministries among the people in the area. Neither a missionary nor a pastor had lived among the Gokwe people for almost eight years. Many of the 40 churches in the vast area had stopped meeting. Church members had backslidden, and many had returned to ancestor worship. We soon realized it would be like starting the work from scratch—all of Gokwe was ripe for the gospel. Once the people learned we were in their area, delegations would visit us and beg us to come to their villages to conduct worship services. By September of that year, Gene had baptized 298 new believers.

Our house was finally finished in June, and we invited the whole countryside to an open house, where we served refreshments. The chief, as well as the church leaders, officially welcomed us to the area, and Gene preached a short sermon. Though this had been a particularly difficult time for us, we were grateful to the Lord for the lessons He had taught us and for the privilege of ministering in this vast, needy area.

---

[1]When speaking of "Gokwe," I usually mean the whole district. But here and in a few other places, it refers to the town called Gokwe.

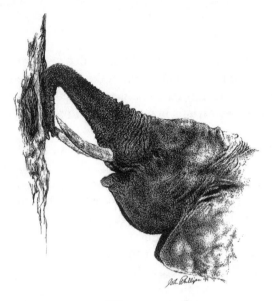

Chapter 8

Receiving God's Blessings

" . . . And the desert shall . . . blossom as the rose; . . .. For waters shall burst forth in the wilderness, . . ."
—Isaiah 35:1, 6 (NKJV).

"The Lord will guide you always; he will satisfy your needs in a sun-scorched land and will strengthen your frame. You will be like a well-watered garden, like a spring whose waters never fail"
—Isaiah 58:11.

Our house at Sasame was situated on a bluff with a valley below. About a mile away in that valley the Tare River snaked to join the Sasame River that was nearer to us. For most of the year, these rivers were dry, but occasionally during the rainy season, they overflowed their banks and flooded the valley. At such times, the roar of the torrents of water made us believe that we lived by the sea.

From our back yard, we could look below to see banana groves and vegetable gardens thriving in the fertile soil of this sandy bottomland. In the distance, we could see lovely hills stretching up the plateau to the small town of Gokwe that bustled with life and growth. Each morning as I looked out of the window, I could imagine the mountains and hills bursting into song and all the trees of the field clapping their hands in praise to our Lord. (See Isaiah 55:12.)

After long years of war and terror, peace had arrived in the valley. We could hear the happy sounds of herd boys playing while their cattle grazed nearby. We loved listening to the laughter of village women as they dug in the sand for water, washed their clothes, or planted, watered, and tended their gardens. Often the prattle of men, women, and children molding mud bricks and burning them floated up to our ears. The nasal, penetrating "*Kweh!*" of the "go away bird" (gray lourie) joined with the harsh cry of the plovers and with the songs of scores of other birds. Added to all this was the loud braying of donkeys, the lowing of cattle, the crowing of proud roosters, and the bleating of goats as they foraged for food. To top this off was the chatter of monkeys swinging in trees as the creatures awaited their opportunity to raid someone's field or our yard.

The delicious aroma of the "potato" tree, that in the evenings smelled like potatoes cooking, and the fragrance of acacia blossoms blended with the smell of smoke from wood fires to give us the scent of rural Africa. On these fires women cooked their *sadza* (thick cornmeal porridge much like sticky rice) and *muriwo* (relish of vegetables or meat).

As we prepared to make our move to the bush, one of the other missionaries asked me, "Jean, what are you going to do without all your flowers and greenery as you go to that dry land of Gokwe? Are you sure you're willing to make this change?"

"Sasame has its own beauty and appeal," I answered. "I've enjoyed God's blessings of beauty in Triangle. However, now that He's called us to Gokwe, I trust Him to give me whatever I need."

One morning soon after that conversation, I read Psalm 37. The words of verse four jumped out at me: "Delight yourself in the Lord and he will give you the desires of your heart."

"Lord, what are you saying to me here? I choose to delight in you and not in a pretty garden. The desires of my heart are to be used of you in bringing people to you. But, Lord, you know how I love pretty flowers, green lawns, and growing things. So I ask you right now to either change these desires or give me some of those wants when we move. I claim this promise from you."

Just in case He was going to make a way to grow things, I began going through my garden and dividing plants, digging up seedlings and small trees, and transplanting them all into containers. When the movers came, they loaded the big flowerpots on their van along with our furniture. We filled our small trailer, which we pulled behind our Toyota pick-up, with the rest of the containers as well as with some of my Australian evergreen lawn.

Among the Louisiana volunteers was a hydrologist who made a study of the Gokwe area. From his studies, he felt certain that artesian water existed underneath the earth in our area. The week we moved to Sasame, his crew was drilling for water. One morning during that first week, the crew members struck water.

I was in the house and heard shouts and lots of commotion nearby. I walked the short distance to where the rig was drilling and saw water oozing up from the ground. As I looked, I realized it was flowing straight toward our yard.

Our garden workers dug a ditch from the site to our yard, and that wonderful water flowed down into what would become our vegetable garden. We planted things, and they began to grow even before our house was finished. However, God still had some more lessons in patience to teach me before all these blessings could be mine.

The volunteers weren't prepared for handling the artesian water when they struck it. And before they could cap it, the drilling rig broke down. Almost a year passed before it was fixed and the water usable. We continued getting water from an old shallow well, which helped me keep my plants alive. Finally a month before the new well was completed, the old well went dry. Now we were completely without water, but for two weeks of this month, God sent rain almost every day. We caught this rain in all available containers. The rest of the time we hauled water from the nearby cotton marketing board.

Finally the rig was repaired and the wonderful day came when, from a depth of 671 feet, water again bubbled up from that artesian well. It flowed at a rate of 57,000 gallons a day. Without a pump, it filled our water tanks; then it was piped into our houses and yards.

Truly, God blessed our garden and our lives through this gift.

We planted fruit trees and vines, oranges, tangerines, lemons, limes, grapefruit, mangoes, guavas, papayas, many types of bananas, mulberries, passion fruit, gooseberries, strawberries, grapes, and pineapples. Within nine months, some of them began to bear fruit. We always had enough for our own needs and plenty to share with others. Better than that, I potted the many seedlings that came up and shared them with our African friends so they, too, would have their own fruit trees.

Year around, we had fresh vegetables for ourselves and for others. Our Australian evergreen lawn thrived and found its way into the courtyard of the clinic and the yards of other mission houses on the station. Eventually people came from other parts of the area and asked for sprigs to plant in their yards. We also had an abundance of beautiful shade trees and shrubs as well as flowers.

The artesian water not only blessed us but also the neighborhood. It was piped to the valley below where the village people no longer had to dig in the sand for water. Now they came to get clean, pure water for their homes and their vegetable gardens in which they grew rape (like collards), cabbage, tomatoes, onions, carrots, and many other good things. These productive gardens fed them year round and were a joy to behold. The volunteers also built convenient places for them to wash their clothes.

Each time the people came to get water, they were reminded of Jesus' words in John 7:37 which were engraved on a sign, "If anyone is thirsty, let him come to me and drink."

The drilling rig was used to drill another artesian well at another clinic about 40 miles from us, as well as to drill numerous other wells throughout the area.

"In a dry and thirsty land, thank you, Lord, for water! Above all, thank you for Jesus, the Living Water!" we said.

PART 4

THE JOURNEY GETS ROUGH

" . . . My grace is sufficient for you, for my power is made perfect in weakness"

—2 Corinthians 12:9.

Lord, the valley is deep and I need your grace
To get me through this, and finish the race.
I'll trust in your promise to work for my good;
Though I don't understand, I'll praise as I should.
                    —Jean Phillips

Chapter 9

What Good Can Come of This?

"And we know that all things work together for good to those who love God, to those who are the called according to His purpose . . . (so they may) be conformed to the image of His Son . . ."
—Romans 8:28-29 (NKJV).

"By the way, Mom and Dad," Mark wrote, "I haven't had a haircut since I left home last August."

It was the last of April, 1973, and our oldest son was trying to prepare us for what we would see when he came home after his first year of college. Earlier in the letter he had written that he didn't plan to return to college in September since he wasn't sure what his major should be and needed a break.

During that year, the Lord had been trying to prepare me for what was happening to our son. Often God would awaken me in the middle of the night with a heavy burden to pray for Mark. The Lord also led me to books about how to pray for and deal with children who were on drugs. I didn't understand my compulsion to read them.

Since the hippie culture and flower children hadn't influenced Rhodesia, nothing could truly prepare me for what I saw when Mark stepped off the plane at the airport in Bulawayo—a young man wearing dirty jeans, faded worn shirt, and a coat that resembled Buffalo Bill's. Thick, curly hair flowing halfway down his back would have been lovely on our daughter Beth, but on our son?

My mind immediately filled with concern and questions. What had happened to Mark during those nine months away from home? He had gone to Chaplin High School in Gwelo, where he lived in the M.K. Home (Missionary Kid's Home). He had worn neat school uniforms and polished shoes. Though he would let his hair grow a bit during the three school holidays each year, when school started, short back and sides were the order of the day. His look now was so totally different, I found the image difficult to digest.

His being away from home during high school prepared me for his absence during college. But his absence did leave an empty spot. When we went to Gwelo for meetings and when the other children came home for holidays, I missed him very much. I had a special burden for Mark because I felt he wasn't truly committed to the Lord. Yes, he had made a profession of faith when he was younger, but my uneasiness lingered.

In the days following Mark's return, I began to sense the reason I'd been reading the books, for I saw in my son all the evidence of drug usage. We began to sense how far he had strayed from God and from what he'd been taught. Selfishness, unbelief, lack of purpose, and Eastern religions all had invaded his life. Eventually we confirmed that our son was also on drugs.

One night while Mark was out of the house, Gene and I, with broken hearts, spent hours crying and asking God what we should do. When he came home, Gene asked Mark to sit down for a talk. When we confronted him with our suspicions, he didn't deny anything. My husband practiced some heart-wrenching tough love by telling our son that we would not allow drugs in our home and that he must get rid of whatever he had. We also reminded him that we loved him and God loved him. I gave him a gospel tract and said, "Son, you know everything in this booklet, but when you decide to do something about your relationship with Christ, this tract will help you return to Him."

During the first few days after his return home, I kept thinking, "What will people think about our son and his appearance?" Then I began thinking, "What will people think when they find out he's on drugs? How many of our friends in the States already know?" I experienced a lot of guilt as I wondered what we had done wrong that caused him to go astray.

In the midst of my anxiety, God began to speak to me through His Word. One morning I read Romans 8:28, and the Lord reminded me of other verses I'd memorized and had begun practicing earlier. God said in Philippians 4:6, "Do not be anxious about anything, but in everything, by prayer and petition, with thanksgiving, present your requests to God." I thought of Ephesians 5:20, "Always giving thanks to God the Father for everything, in the name of our Lord Jesus Christ." I also thought of 1 Thessalonians 5:18, "Give thanks in all circumstances, for this is God's will for you in Christ Jesus."

Then I argued with God: "Lord, surely you don't expect me to thank you in this. What good can you possibly bring out of this?"

God assured me I was to praise and thank Him and trust Him to use all this in Mark's life and ours for our good and His glory.

I whined, "But God, you said in Proverbs 22:6, 'Train a child in the way he should go, and when he is old he will not turn from it.'"

At that moment, the Lord showed me what I had never seen before in that verse. The phrase, "when he is old," jumped out at me, and I seemed to hear the Lord saying, "He might go astray, but if you honor me, he'll come back." Then I remembered this poem I had written nine months before as Mark left for college:

What does a mother feel when her son leaves for college 8,000 miles away,
  In a world of materialism and rebellion,
  Of hippies, drugs, sex, crime, and wrong values,
  In a selfish world which forgets God?

What does she feel when her 18-year-old
  Leaves his world of disciplined school-life,
  Khaki uniforms, blazer, basher, and gray flannels,
  His hobbies, his friends, his dogs, and her?

She feels anxiety and worry,
Loneliness and fear,
Sadness, helplessness,
and gratitude.

Gratitude to God who has promised
That if she has trained, her son won't depart,
If she will commit, He will keep,
If she will ask, He will answer,
If she will beg, He will give,
If she will trust, He will sustain.

She has sought to train all these years,
She has committed long ago,
She has asked many times,
She will continue to beg, and trust,
   And God will cause her heart to feel peace.

Now I pondered, "Where was my peace now? Why had it fled? Was God not faithful?" On my knees that morning, I confessed my own sin. I was feeling sorry for myself and was having pity parties again. My eyes had strayed from my Lord and were fixated on problems and situations. My focus had shifted to thoughts such as, "Mark will bring disgrace to our ministry."

I prayed, "Forgive me, Father, for being so self-centered. Forgive me for not trusting in you. Lord, Gene and I gave Mark to you when he was conceived, then when he was born. Now I give him to You once again. You can take him anywhere or do anything You need to do with him. You can drag our reputation in the mud if it takes that to bring glory to Your Name. In myself I'm not able to thank and praise You for all this, but I'm willing for You to make me willing to do this."

Then as a sheer act of obedience, I said, "Lord, I thank and praise You for Mark just as he is."

I rose from my knees with the peace of God flooding my heart and mind once again. I knew Mark was completely out of my hands. I was free to love him with Christ's unselfish love. And that's just what happened. My heart began to overflow with love for him.

That day also marked the turning point in Mark's life. He started to open up and talk to his dad and me. With our human lines of communication open, he opened up to what God had to say to him, too. And soon God freed him of bad habits and brought about renewal and healing in his life.

Mark chose to continue his education at Columbia Bible College (CBC; now Columbia International University) in Columbia, SC, where he graduated *magna cum laude* in 1976. While there, his past experiences caused him to have a concern for the juvenile delinquents in a home where he ministered.

Years later, I now see the truth of Romans 8:28 in this situation. If his life had not been messed up, Mark probably would not have attended CBC and thus would not have met the precious girl God brought into his life while there. Janice Tuggy, the younger sister of two of Mark's classmates and a missionary kid from Venezuela, later became Mark's wife. Because of his ministry to juvenile delinquents, he had a desire to work in the rehabilitation of prisoners. God led him into teaching vocational carpentry to inmates in Columbia, SC. He now quips, "I've done 17 years hard time behind bars."

Today, we are very proud of our first-born and his wonderful family, consisting of wife Janice, son Danny, who is a senior in college, and twin daughters, Robin and April, who are freshmen in college. A high point in each of our lives occurred in 1994 when Mark and his family visited in Zimbabwe for six weeks. This was Mark's first trip back to Africa since he left to enter CBC in 1973. In Zimbabwe, Mark and 14-year-old Danny did some much needed carpentry work on the mission station, while the twins painted and helped in other ways. They all participated in church services, made friends, witnessed, and played soccer with the Africans. Janice's greatest contribution came through teaching literacy and coaching some of our youth in English. Out of this group, several went on to take the English course at the Zimbabwe Baptist Seminary. Today one of them, Philip Mudzidzi, is pastor of an English-speaking Baptist church in Harare. Another, Luckson Chiombera, is pastor of a church in Gweru.

Prior to their arrival in Africa, the 11-year-old twins had not made a profession of faith. Gene and I had been praying for them. When I was talking to April about the need to make this decision, I realized she was ready to do so. So, I led her in the sinner's prayer and suggested that she go tell her family what she had done. Happily, she professed Christ before them. The next day Gene had the privilege of leading Robin to accept Christ. Today, when the girls talk about their trip to Africa, they say the best part was that during their time there, they both accepted Christ.

Chapter 10

The Sacrifice of Praise

"When anxiety was great within me, your consolation brought joy to my soul"
                                                                    —Psalm 94:19.

"Through Jesus, therefore, let us continually offer to God a sacrifice of praise . . . "
                                                                    —Hebrews 13:15.

"He who sacrifices thank offerings honors me . . ."
                                                                    —Psalm 50:23

The loud ring of the telephone jarred us awake on the night of February 1, 1983. It was not good news. Our second son, John, had experienced a mental breakdown and had been hospitalized.

God had taught me much through John already. Though very intelligent and gifted in art, as a child John had a difficult time learning to read. School was a great effort for him. On our second furlough, we took him for psychological testing. The psychologist told me I was an anxious mother who was just comparing him with his older brother. But it hurt to see him berated in school for his slowness to learn when I knew he was very capable. A placid child with a sweet disposition, John began to struggle with his self-image.

Finally on a furlough when John was 11, his wonderful sixth-grade teacher recognized a definite problem and sent him for tests at the Orton Reading Center in Winston-Salem, NC. After testing, we were told John had dyslexia. With a huge sigh of relief, my first words were, "You mean there's a name for it?"

I had majored in elementary education in college but had never heard of this learning disorder, which is diagnosed routinely today. Back then, however, it was often undiagnosed and untreated. Mrs. Orton, whose husband founded the center based on his ground-breaking research, gave me exercises to do with John to help him learn some of the basics that he needed. All during the summer of that furlough, John worked diligently to overcome his handicap and catch up on his schoolwork. With much patience and effort, by the time we returned to Rhodesia, John had made significant progress and was ready to enter high school.

High schools in Rhodesia at that time used the British system of education. This system focused on what was called "streams of learning." John was placed in the non-academic stream where the emphasis was more on practical subjects. He often felt cheated when he compared his studies with those of his siblings. But his abilities in art helped to compensate for some of what he wasn't getting as he struggled through three years of high school.

On our next furlough, because of the difference in the educational systems, John was a junior in high school. He did very well in regular courses in the States and enjoyed his studies. In April, 1975, when we returned to Rhodesia from that furlough, we were excited about the prospects of his continuing to make progress. But soon we were brought back to the reality of the Rhodesian system of education for slower learners. We began to realize it would be best if John returned to the States for his senior year of high school. This was certainly not our first choice, but it seemed to be the best option. Subsequently, we began half-heartedly to investigate this possibility.

In all honesty, I procrastinated on taking action because I wanted to put off as long as possible his leaving us. Then suddenly in mid-September, two weeks before John's 18th birthday, a new problem that had been simmering bubbled over into a frightening reality.

Because of Rhodesia's civil war, all 17-year-old white males in the country were required to register for the draft. They then could be called into the Rhodesian army at 18. Since we had been back from furlough only a few months, we hadn't considered the full significance of this law upon our own children. John, however, had been concerned about it and kept reminding us of the law. His friends all asked him when he was going into the army to help defend the country against Communism.

That day in September, we dropped off John, Beth, and Paul at the M.K. Home in Gwelo to begin their third term of school. Then we drove to Baptist Camp to spend the night before heading home the next day. It was there we heard some disturbing news and came face-to-face with the new reality confronting us. A few months earlier, another Missionary Kid John's age had received his call-up papers. He and his father immediately made an appointment to talk with the proper official. They explained that the son had been accepted for college and already had his ticket to leave for the States in August before his 18th birthday. The official wrote a letter giving that young man permission to leave the country. After he returned to the States, his parents heard that some of his school friends didn't think it was fair for him to leave when they had to go into the army. They also learned these school friends had reported to the government authorities that their son was leaving in August to get out of army duty, which was why his call-up papers arrived early.

As missionaries and American citizens, we had to stay neutral in Rhodesia's political problems. We felt that neither we nor our children could serve in Rhodesia's armed forces without damaging the purposes of our being there in the first place. Consequently, we knew our only recourse was to send John out of the country before he turned 18, and we knew he had to go immediately!

Distraught, and not ready for this, I cried out to God, "Lord, we don't know where to send him. You know he's not ready to leave home. He has so much he needs to learn in order to survive on his own. After what happened to Mark, how can we let him go? Please give us strength and wisdom."

As we tried to decide what to do, Gene and I began to talk and pray. Because of what had happened to the other missionary kid, we felt John needed to leave quietly without telling his friends he was going.

Thankfully, God was already at work on a solution. At that very time, some friends from the States were in Gwelo and planning to return to Triangle with us the next day for a visit before they left for Johannesburg. We discussed the situation with them and with other missionaries and decided that John should travel with our friends to Johannesburg. Once there, he would stay with another missionary family until we could work out the next step.

We phoned our dear friends and co-workers, Bud and Jane Fray in Johannesburg, and arranged for John to stay with them. We prayed the rest of the night, then at daybreak, drove to the M.K. Home. There we quietly gathered John, Beth, and Paul and explained the situation to them. We told them that John must not enroll for third term, that he needed to leave without telling his friends, and that I would write a letter to the school's headmaster explaining that he was going to finish his education in the States.

John expressed relief. We prayed together with our children, sent the two younger ones to school, and helped John get his possessions together. Then the three of us, along with our friends from the U.S., headed back to Triangle. I continued to pack for John, while Gene escorted our friends around the area. Two days later, John and the friends left for Johannesburg.

At that time, Mark was attending Columbia Bible College. We phoned him about all that was transpiring. We asked him to work with our family consultant, Truman Smith, at the Foreign Mission Board to find a school for John. Truman recommended Harrison Chilhowee Baptist Academy in Tennessee. The school gladly accepted John, and we purchased his airline ticket to return to the States.

The last week of September, Gene, Beth, Paul, and I drove to Johannesburg to celebrate John's birthday, do some fun things together as a family, and give John some last-minute instructions before putting him on the plane for the U.S. This experience was traumatic for us, but John seemed to take it in stride.

On arrival in the U.S., Mark met John at the airport and drove him to school. John seemed to adjust well to his new environment. He did well in all his studies, but he excelled in art. He won a prize for one of his pictures, made friends among faculty as well as students, and graduated in May, 1976.

The following September John entered Wingate College, where he studied art for two years at this small North Carolina Baptist school. While a student, he was hired to paint a mural at a shopping mall in Charlotte, NC. In September, 1978, he transferred to the University of North Carolina at Greensboro, where he caught up on foreign language study, which he had not taken in high school. We were quite proud of him when he received the Bachelor of Fine Arts degree in May, 1982! That same week, his sister Beth graduated *summa cum laude* from Gardner Webb College with a major in physics with chemistry.

John found college to be very stressful. During his years at UNC-G, we suggested several times that he change to a commercial art college. He refused to change and was determined to get his degree. My feelings are expressed in the following poem, which I wrote at the time of his graduation.

I wonder if you know, Son,
How proud we are of you,
That though the load's been heavy,
You've seen your studies through.

Today's your graduation,
A dream impossible,
Or so it seemed some years back
When still in grammar school.

For when you were a youngster,
It was so very hard
To learn the words so simple,
Though offered a reward.

We cried and were frustrated;
You were intelligent,

But somehow things so easy
Didn't seem to make a dent.

Then one day we discovered
('Twas the Lord who gave insight)
Dyslexia was your handicap
And hope was brought to light.

We learned you'd have to work hard,
But you could overcome
Your handicap with much effort,
To get your work all done.

And now this day you've proven
That hard work really pays,
For you have stuck it out, Son,
Through dreary nights and days.

You've taught us all a lesson
And you have won a fight,
Through God's own strength and power,
You've proved His way is right.

Still, oft I've questioned Jesus
As to why you had to bear
A load so very heavy.
I've asked Him, "Do you care?"

He's shown me very clearly
That He is teaching you
To have patience and compassion,
And trust in all you do.

So though you've won a victory,
The fight has just begun;
You've got to keep on working,
And life's race you've got to run.

Trust Jesus for your future,
Seek His will in all you do,
Let Him fill you with His Spirit,
And live His life through you.

We took a three-month furlough in May, 1982, to attend the two graduations. While in the States, I saw signs of depression in John. He had deep scars and resentments toward us in many areas. In the grownup world of job, housing, and bills, he was finding it hard to cope. We encouraged him to seek help from a Christian counselor, but he declined. At the same time, we helped him move into a mobile home in Greensboro, where he was working. Then we returned to Zimbabwe at the end of August. Beth lived in the mobile home with him until the end of December, 1982. At that time, she left the States to teach Science at Sanyati Baptist High School in Zimbabwe, where she later became head of the Science Department.

Then came that frightening, middle-of-the-night phone call the following February when we, in Triangle, were beginning to think about our move to Gokwe. The days after that call were like a nightmare, so I quickly booked a flight to the States to be with John.

He was diagnosed as manic-depressive and given Lithium. It broke my heart to see him confused and psychotic. Eventually he seemed to stabilize and was released from the hospital. He wanted to return to Zimbabwe with me. So a month later we both flew back to Africa.

John seemed very happy to be home. He related well to Ron Fannin, a Journeyman working with youth in our area. But John didn't like to take his medicine, and after six weeks had a relapse. He was hospitalized in the capital city of Harare (formerly Salisbury), 300 miles from Triangle. His Zimbabwe doctor diagnosed him as "bipolar schizophrenic." This doctor changed John's medicine numerous times as he tried to find the right combination that would correct John's chemical imbalance. At one point, while in a manic state, John climbed over a wall at the hospital and was missing 23 hours. After walking 25 miles, he eventually found his way back to the hospital. Following many setbacks, he was finally released from the hospital in September.

John stayed in Zimbabwe for the next two years. Though he had a number of relapses, he also experienced some good times. In February, 1984, we moved to Gokwe, and he stayed busy painting and working on the houses, as well as drawing. During that time, he finished four fantastic pen-and-ink drawings of African animals in pointillism style. He was halfway through his fifth one of two elephants fighting when he had his worst relapse up to that time. This was the hardest episode for Gene and me to accept, since he had done so well, and we had believed God was healing him.

One night when John was in a manic state, Gene and I cried until we had no more tears left. Finally, we said to each other, "Let's sing and praise the Lord." Through our tears, we lifted our cracking voices up to God and offered Him a sacrifice of praise. Praise got us through the night, and the next day we made the long trip back to the hospital with John.

Because of John's more frequent hospitalizations, in June 1985 we took a four-month furlough so John again could receive stateside medical help. Since Mark lived in Columbia, SC, we were happy to learn that First Baptist Church of Camden, SC, 33 miles from Columbia, had an available missionary house. We liked South Carolina's mental health department, as well as Columbia's mental health facilities and doctors.

Though we prayed, cried, begged, and claimed God's healing and deliverance, it seemed that God did not choose to bring about a quick "fix" for John. Our furlough was extended and finally became a leave of absence. During the 13 months we lived in their missionary house, our wonderful church ministered to us. The church loved John, and members visited him in the hospital. The church prayed with us and for us and helped us through one of the most difficult times in our lives.

After we went on leave of absence, we knew we had to decide what we would do next. Did God want Gene to accept a pastorate in the States? If He wanted us back in Zimbabwe, what arrangements would we make for John when he was out of hospital?

One day we decided to go aside for prayer. We went to a nearby state park. Gene went one way with his Bible, and I went another with mine. We agreed to come back together after about three hours alone with the Lord. At the appointed time, we met to find out what God had said to us individually.

When we compared experiences, we realized God had given both of us a fresh call to missions! So we joined hands and prayed together, saying, "God, we're willing to trust you with John and go back to the field." Then we added, "But please, Lord, will you confirm three times what you're saying to us?"

We went home. As we walked in the door, the phone was ringing. A dear friend from First Baptist had a word from the Lord during her Quiet Time that morning and felt it was for us. "Cast your bread upon the waters, for after many days you will find it again" (Ecc. 11:1). God seemed to be saying, "I want you to go across the waters to give out the Bread of Life, for it will bear fruit."

The next confirmation came from our Mission Board, which signaled it would stand behind whatever decision we made.

The third confirmation came from John's psychiatrist. He knew we had been in a holding pattern for some time. He said to us one day, "You folks need to face the fact that your son is chronically ill, and your being with him will not help him get better. You need to get on with your lives."

With that third confirmation, we prayed, "Thank you, Lord! Thank you for making it clear that we are to return to Zimbabwe. We trust you to care for John as we obey you."

We booked our flights for June, 1986, two weeks after that third confirmation. Before flying out of the Columbia airport, we went by the hospital to say goodbye to John. He was in a catatonic state and gave no acknowledgement of our presence. But we talked to him as though he could hear us and told him we loved him and were returning to our work in Zimbabwe. Amid our tears, we kissed him goodbye. Then with heavy hearts, made glad through obedience and praise of our Lord, we boarded the plane. We looked forward to what our faithful God was going to do as we trusted Him and obeyed. We knew He would rescue this situation somehow. And God was faithful! John began improving as soon as we left. Soon he was out of hospital and living in a mental health halfway house.

We went to the States on a month's vacation in July, 1987, for Beth's wedding. John was well enough to serve as an usher. Then while we were on a furlough in 1992, his doctors decided to try a new medicine. This has stabilized him to such a degree that during the ten years he's been on it (up to the time of writing this book), he has been hospitalized only three times. These were times he felt the need to regulate his dosage under hospital care.

John lives in a mental health apartment complex in Columbia, SC, where he is "resident artist" and has a ministry of caring for others. Recently he said to me, "Mom, you know, I can praise God for my sickness, for through it, I understand many with whom I live. I can talk to them when they are discouraged, and I can tell them how to trust God to care for them." John meets with some of his friends in the complex for Bible study, and they go to church together on Sundays. He has a passion to see the lost saved.

We're very proud of John and are most grateful to the Lord for the way He's worked in our son's life. He is a blessing to us and to many others. Our Zimbabwe Baptist Publishing House made prints of his animal drawings—the giraffe, lion with cub, cheetah running, kudu, and elephants. (Since then, he has done others.) We chose verses depicting the characteristic of each animal, and these verses are printed on the pictures. The Publishing House also printed Scripture notelets featuring his animals with their verses. John's art is blessing people all over the world. May it bless you as you see it in this book on the introductory page of each chapter.

In 1988, four years after it was begun, John finished his elephants fighting picture. (It is at the beginning of chapters 3 and 15.) The verse we chose for that one is, "But thanks be to God! He gives us the victory through our Lord Jesus Christ" (1 Cor. 15:57). We can testify to the truth of that verse throughout the many battles we have encountered in our lives. God, through Christ, is the one who gives victory.

PART 5

DAILY LIFE

"Therefore I tell you, do not worry about your life . . . .Who of you by worrying can add a single hour to his life? . . . .But seek first his (God's) kingdom and his righteousness, and all these things will be given to you as well"

—Matthew 6:25, 27, 33.

Chapter 11

The Gift of Laughter

"Our mouths were filled with laughter, our tongues with songs of joy . . ."
—Psalm 126:2.

"A cheerful heart is good medicine . . . "
—Proverbs 17:22.

I didn't grow up laughing at things that went wrong. I could laugh at funny stories but didn't often see the funny side of problems. Gene, however, joked a lot and helped teach me to laugh at situations as well as at myself. Soon after we arrived in Rhodesia, I found that a sense of humor was essential to survival. In this chapter, I share with you the humor in some very difficult circumstances.

* * * * *

We were living in the small asbestos mining town of Shabani. It was the dry season, and fresh vegetables were difficult to find. One day, I went to the store and found all the ingredients for a wonderful, fresh tossed salad. I could almost taste it as I took from the refrigerator the crisp lettuce, bell pepper, tomatoes, celery, and carrots. Having other things to do, I gave these things to Rebecca, our maid, and told her to prepare them. I showed her how to cut them up, then left the room.

Suddenly, in the midst of my duties, I sniffed the air. "Is that bell pepper I'm smelling?" I wondered. "Why is Rebecca cooking bell pepper? B-b-bell pepper? Oh, no-o-o, my salad!!"

I went to the kitchen to find my lovely tossed salad boiling away on the stove.

I couldn't scold Rebecca, because I hadn't told her what to do with the vegetables when she had prepared them. And until then, she had only cooked the food she had prepared. So I laughed, and all my irritation vanished. I then used this concoction as a base for soup.

* * * * *

As a teenager, Paul, our youngest son, found that a sense of humor helped him in a game of golf. A great golf course was situated on the Triangle Sugar Estates. We could use the course without cost. The third green, a short hole, was beside a river. Paul made a beautiful, one-shot drive that landed near the hole. As he walked up to make his putt, a monkey ran from a tree, grabbed the ball, and climbed back up the tree with his prize. Finding that it wasn't food, the monkey threw it in the river.

* * * * *

When Paul and his wife Shana came to visit us after their marriage in 1993, laughter "saved the day" for Shana, though not her hair. Soon after their arrival, she was in the bedroom when I smelled a strong scent of singed hair. Holding her curling iron in one hand and a handful of hair in the other, Shana entered the room where I was. She explained that she had used the wrong adapter on her 110-volt curling iron. Although the curling iron worked on our 220-volt electricity, it overheated and burnt off her bangs. She had to develop a new hairstyle until her bangs grew out again.

* * * * *

In our latter years on the field when we lived at Sasame, it was a bit more difficult to laugh at some of the everyday problems. Since we generated our own electricity on the station, and the generator only ran about three or four hours at night, we had to use a gas refrigerator, freezer, and stove. Gas refrigerators don't have compressors, so every time we opened the door, the hot air rushed in and the cold air out. Meat would sometimes spoil, and on occasion we even found ants in the refrigerator. The most frustrating thing about the gas refrigerator was when the gases didn't circulate properly and the refrigerator warmed up. To solve that problem, we had to remove everything, take the refrigerator outside, turn it upside down and "burp" it. After leaving it that way a day or so, we could bring it back into the house and hook it up. Usually within 24 hours it worked properly again.

My attitude toward this situation with the refrigerator required much prayer, and we asked God to help us find a more efficient appliance. Nevertheless, it was impossible to find a refrigerator larger than about 10 cubic feet, with three cubic feet of freezing space, so we usually had two. That way, we hoped to have at least one that was running.

Our deep freeze did well in the winter months. But in the summer, for the most part, it served as a very cold refrigerator.

While in the States in 1986, we located a much improved gas refrigerator. We shipped it, and it arrived safely. But while in Zimbabwe customs, the officials opened the crate and pulled back the plastic we had used to cover the contents. To keep the plastic out of their way, they fastened it to the top of the crate with a huge nail that went through plastic, the crate, into the top of our fridge— right into the freezone pipe! Eventually it was fixed and worked well until 1990. One day it wasn't as cold as usual. A few hours later we noticed a terrible, ammonia-like smell. We had to buy a new unit from the States. The new unit took months to deliver. But we finally had a good refrigerator!

In the midst of all my refrigerator ordeals, I eventually learned to laugh and thank God for what we had.

* * * * *

We mistakenly purchased our gas stove with an electronic oven thermostat. Since the stove could not be hooked up to electricity and consequently had no working thermostat, baking was a real challenge. I often said, "It's better to laugh over a burnt cake, pie, cornbread, biscuits, or cookies than to cry!" When visitors were coming and my cake burned, I learned to laugh as well as to say, "Praise the Lord!"

* * * * *

Our generator was another irritation. We used it three or four hours each night and about an hour during the day once a week so that the clinic could process blood slides. We took advantage of that hour of extra electricity to wash clothes, iron, vacuum, and do other tasks with our appliances. When the generator broke down, which was often, we had to wait weeks for someone to arrive from town and fix it.

The Sasame Baptist Church pastor, Clement Chipunza, whom the Lord saved and called to preach under our ministry at Triangle, had a real knack for repairing things. We rejoiced when he learned to repair the generator!

* * * * *

Once on my birthday, when someone suggested a candlelight dinner, we said "No, thank you! We've been without electricity for weeks, and now we have lights. We've had enough candles for a while!"

* * * * *

We had a coal iron and an electric iron. The bottom of the coal iron opened up, and embers were put inside. We had no way to regulate the temperature, so things sometimes were scorched. It wasn't easy to laugh the day a piece was burned out of my favorite blouse.

* * * * *

Septic tanks also were a challenge. Ours caved in twice, and we had to put up with foul odors and no toilet facilities for about two weeks until it was rebuilt.

* * * * *

Another time laughing was a bit more difficult. We discovered one day that the reason our water had tasted strange for about two weeks was that two squirrels had somehow taken a suicide dive into our covered water tank. Yuk! How they got into the tank remains a mystery. We drained the tank, cleaned and sterilized it thoroughly, aired it, and finally refilled it.

* * * * *

We heated our water by building a fire under a 44-gallon drum of water. The hot water was then piped into the house. Our workers didn't work on weekends, so since we were usually too busy at that time to build the fire, we learned to get along without hot water and to do it with a "smile." Smiling wasn't so easy when the drum rusted and developed a hole. We were without hot water until we could locate a new drum, clean it of airplane fuel odors, and hook it up. Eventually we got a stronger tank that wouldn't rust.

* * * * *

Through the years our dogs gave us much joy. In 1987, I wrote in our family report to the mission about our fabulous family festivities, fertile fields, and fraternal fellowship. Then I added:

"We wish we didn't have to mention our frequent frustrations, but to tell the whole story, we must. Causing many of these were our four furry friends of the canine variety. Two puppies plotted to bring us to financial ruin and nervous exhaustion by their frequent illnesses and destructive tactics. Returning from a month in the States, we discovered that faithful 13-year-old Pointer Rex had breathed his last breath. It was great having Fat Fundi (our Lab) keep some semblance of order in this crazy canine world.

"Add to these frivolous annoyances the broken down refrigerators, freezers, generators and trucks, broken water pipes, caved in septic tanks, multitudinous mosquitoes, sly snakes (including our neighbor, the python), and the everpresent knock on the door."

In all these things God was working on me so His light would shine out of me despite the irritations of life.

* * * * *

Learning to eat what was served us in African homes and meetings sometimes taxed every bit of our sense of humor. I managed quite well with most of the foods except *mahewo*, a drink made from corn meal and sugar. A different blend of this which they fermented was the local beer or *doro* that many Africans drank. But *mahewo* was neither fermented nor intoxicating and was safe to drink since it had been cooked well. My problem with it occurred when I got it in my mouth and rolled it around on my tongue. The grainy, thick liquid just wouldn't go down. Since they served it at most church meals, weddings, funerals and community affairs, I developed all kinds of ways of avoiding it. These ranged from pretending to drink to taking a sip then excusing myself to go outside and get rid of it in the best way possible. Finally, I found out that it was OK to decline, and our friends would usually offer me hot tea or a soda.

Gene found a humorous way to get around some of his dislikes. At weekend leadership meetings, the Africans usually killed a goat to serve with their *sadza*. (*Sadza* was their staple food which they ate every day of their lives.) They always gave their visitors the choice parts of the goat—the stomach, intestines, heart, or liver. Fortunately, I like liver, and once the nationals learned to serve me only liver, my problem with these meals was resolved. It wasn't so easy for Gene! Neither liver nor the other "delicacies" ranked anywhere on his "I-like" list.

The Africans have a superstition concerning their clan name, or *mutupo*. If their *mutupo* was *Moyo* (heart), they were not supposed to eat the heart of any animal. If it was *nyathi* (buffalo), they could not eat buffalo, and so on. We asked what would happen if they ate their *mutupo*. They said, "Oh, our teeth will fall out, or something very bad will happen to us."

Gene often joked with them, so they understood what he meant when he said, "My *mutupo* is *chiropa* (liver). If I eat it, my hair will turn white." And of course, his hair was already white by the time he learned this trick. So they all had a good laugh and gave him goat meat stew, which he ate while I devoured my boiled *chiropa*.

* * * * *

When Gene or I began to take things too seriously or worried about what might happen in a situation, we had a little story that helped us laugh and lighten up.

"A man named George needed to borrow his neighbor's jack. As he was walking over to neighbor Jim's house, George began to think, 'Jim may not be at home. He may be asleep or busy.' He walked on, and the thought came to him, 'He may be using his jack, or he may not lend it to me.'

"As he neared Jim's house, he remembered, 'The last time I asked to borrow something from Jim, he was impatient with me.'

"When right at Jim's door, George thought, 'Why, Jim may beat me up if I ask to borrow his jack.' He turned on his heel, threw a rock at the house, and said, 'Just keep your old jack. I don't need it anyway.' "

Sometimes just the words, "Just keep your old jack", spoken by either Gene or me would avert an argument or change a disagreement into a time of laughter.

We've learned that when we shine with Christ's light, laughter occurs.

Chapter 12

Coping with African Creatures

"How many are your works, O Lord! In wisdom you made them all; the earth is full of your creatures"
—Psalm 104:24.

"God created man in his own image . . . and said . . . 'Rule over . . . every living creature . . ."
—Genesis 1:27-28

Africa and bugs go together like ice cream and cake. Bugs of all descriptions live there and take up residence everywhere possible. Take, for instance, weevils who live in flour, in corn meal, in dried beans, in dog meal, or in any other foodstuff they fancy and can get into. Flying bugs that come out at night in the summertime are also in abundance. No matter how well screened our houses were, these creatures found their way into our dwellings and flew to the lights. When the season arrived for the tiny biting midge, the greasy round bug, or the flying ant (termite), we often chose to sit in the dark rather than have these creatures invade us to get to the light.

Our youngest child, Paul, loved flying ant season. He was truly a child of Africa and savored these African delicacies! These termites build anthills that sometimes are as big as an African hut. During the dry season, Africans "fish" for ants by sticking a long wet reed into the tunnels they find in these giant anthills. Being thirsty, the ants latch onto the reed; then the Africans rake them off into a container and take them home to cook for supper.

When the rains arrive and flood their tunnels, the termites fly out of their homes and to outside lights. When this occurred, Paul, along with our African neighbors, gathered these delicacies for dinner the next day. Sometimes Paul ate his fill of fried ants and then froze some for later.

Because of the termites, we built our cement block or brick houses on a cement slab. If a break occurred in the slab, termites found their way to any wood in the house. One night soon after we moved into our relatively new house in Shabani, I heard a noise. While in language school in Salisbury, I had heard such a noise in a very old mission house. I was told it was termites. So I told Gene I could hear termites in our Shabani house. He laughed at me and said it was impossible to hear them.

I didn't argue but followed the sound and stopped where I thought they were. Pointing, I said, "They're right here." When Gene touched the wooden baseboard where I pointed, his finger went right through it. Nothing was left but a shell.

Some of our bugs were quite large. One night in Triangle, as a visiting evangelist stood up to preach in our multiracial, interdenominational crusade, a huge moth began flying around him. He tried stepping on it, but it flew away. He scooted after it in the direction of the choir. It flew straight to a European woman who could not tolerate such creatures. She let out a piercing scream and fled through the open doors behind her. That bug nearly broke up our worship service!

We had all kinds of flies, too. The maggot fly laid eggs in wet clothing. If a person later wore these clothes, these eggs hatched into maggots, which bored into his or her skin and caused a boil-like swelling that would have to be removed. Because of this, we had to iron everything that was hung outside. The heat from the iron killed the maggots.

One day, when John was a baby, we noticed a boil on his ear.

When we squeezed out what we thought was the core of the boil, it started wiggling. We knew that somehow a fly had laid its egg on our baby's sheet, and we learned first-hand about maggots. Once it was out, John was fine.

Parasitic worms called Schistosomes were in rivers, streams, or any body of water where their snail host lived. When a person entered such infected water, he or she ran the risk of becoming infected with the parasite and developing a disease called bilharzia. If untreated, this disease can be very serious and affects the bladder or the bowels. Most Africans have had bilharzia at one time or the other. Gene contracted it when he baptized in the rivers but was treated and had no ill effects.

Mosquitoes were another kind of problem, since during most of our years on the field, we lived in hot, low-lying malaria areas, with the malaria-carrying anopheles mosquitoes in abundance. In Triangle, the health department kept malaria under control by giving all Triangle employees, as well as us, weekly prophylactic drugs. So we never had malaria while we lived there.

It was a different story when we moved to Gokwe. We continued taking our weekly preventatives, but the people around us didn't, and malaria was rampant in the area. Since the patients arrived for treatment at our Baptist clinic a few hundred yards from our house, mosquitoes that bit them also bit us. We were bitten in our many outside night meetings and when we camped out while doing ministry. When the mosquitoes became immune to the drugs we used, we then began contracting malaria.

Our missionary co-laborer, nurse Mary Louise Clark, often did the work of a doctor. Malaria can be very debilitating, and she cared for us when we were ill. She tried different drugs to help cure our bouts with malaria. Once, however, Gene nearly died from a severe case that wouldn't respond to any of her treatments. By God's providence, at the time Gene was so ill, a Mission Aviation Fellowship plane was at Sasame to fly us to a remote area of ministry. Instead of taking us to do ministry, the plane flew us to Harare, where Gene was hospitalized.

That was the year when many people, even in the higher altitude, cooler climate of Harare, died from malaria. But God mercifully protected Gene in spite of his raging fever, bone-breaking aches, nausea, vomiting, and serious condition. Our dear friend and brother in the Lord, Dr. Chris Nutt, was Gene's physician at the time. He had been our doctor in Triangle for many years and had been saved in that wonderful revival during the war. People prayed for Gene, and after many different treatments over a period of almost a week in the hospital, God healed my husband. Once again, God's rescue was evident in our lives.

Because of the many mosquitoes, we were grateful for the geckos (lizards) that lived in our house and ate them. In 1969, my mother visited us in Triangle. Soon after her arrival, I heard loud noises emerging from her room. When I investigated, I found her trying to eliminate these "friendly" roommates. I said, "Mama, we don't kill geckos. They help us by eating flies and mosquitoes."

Back in the States, she told about geckos as one adjustment she had to make to life in Africa. A few years later, a pastor's wife who heard her story visited us. Walking into her bedroom, she saw the geckos on the wall. Trying to reassure herself, she said, "These do belong here, don't they?"

We once experienced a plague of rats in the Gokwe area. This occurred when a long, devastating drought killed many snakes. Snakes eat rats, so when the snakes died, the rats flourished. This is one of the ways of nature.

The drought also impacted the food production of the Africans. Since they were now hungry, and since they eat rats, the Africans found ways to catch the expanding number of rats. Our garden worker dug a hole in our garden and placed in the hole, level with the ground, a bucket half full of water. Then he rigged up a stick across the top of the bucket and dangled a pod of okra, spread with peanut butter, from the stick. The rats arrived for the food and fell into the water. One night, the gardener caught 100 rats that way. He and his family had plenty of protein that day!

Once a mouse got into our car and chewed the wires to our radio. Weeks passed before we managed to catch him. Another time one got into our gas stove and began pulling out the insulation from around the burners. We set traps, but that intelligent, "educated" mouse ate the bait without setting off the trap. She used the insulation to build a nest in the back of our stove. Not until Gene tied the bait on the spring did we finally catch that creature.

Our first experience with scorpions occurred while we lived in the farmhouse near Triangle. Mark got up one morning and put on his shoes to get ready for school. When he screamed, we found that a huge scorpion had claimed his shoe during the night. When Mark wanted his shoe back, the scorpion put up a fight to keep its new home. Another one crawled in bed with John and stung him. Scorpions frequently made their presence known when we moved into the small workers' quarters at Triangle. We learned always to check our shoes before putting them on. We also learned that the big ones aren't the most poisonous. Though their stings hurt, the effects of these big ones soon went away.

While living at Sasame, I awoke one night feeling something crawling on my neck. I brushed it off and experienced a terrible, painful sting on my finger. As I cried out, Gene awoke and turned on his flashlight to search for the culprit. He found a tiny, light brown scorpion on the floor where I had flung it after my sting. We found out that this was one of the more poisonous kinds, as the pain, swelling, and numbness in that finger for the next 10 days proved.

Out of all the creatures with which we had to cope, snakes were the least liked. My first experience with snakes occurred while we lived in the asbestos mining town of Shabani the year after we arrived in Africa. One day our gardener, Titus, reported a huge snake among some rocks in the garden. Gene was not home, so I decided this was the time to put into practice what he had taught me the year before about shooting snakes. I didn't grow up with guns as Gene had. I didn't know the difference between a rifle, a shotgun, or a .458 elephant gun, all of which Gene owned. I went to the gun cabinet and deliberated, "Hmmm, which one am I supposed to use? And how do I load it?"

Grabbing what I thought was the right one, I selected some ammunition. Then I headed for the garden, where Titus was waiting. He showed me the snake's head just sticking out from among the rocks. I cocked the gun, aimed it, and, thinking I'd try it out, pulled the trigger. I looked around to ask Titus to check and see if I'd hit the snake, but Titus was nowhere to be seen. I thought, "Oh no! Did I shoot him instead of the snake?" I ran to the worker's quarters in the back and found him peeping out from around the corner, frightened out of his wits by the blast of the gun. Titus was fine, but wonder of wonders, the snake was dead!

Snakes sometimes appeared at church both at Triangle and in Gokwe. One Sunday, in a church building made out of poles with a thatched roof, one of the lay preachers was preaching about Moses lifting up the serpent in the wilderness. While making his point, he looked up. Above him on the rafters was a huge cobra. He stopped the service, while some of the men helped him kill the snake. Then, with the deed done, they continued with their worship service.

When we moved to Sasame, we were surrounded by bush that the snakes had claimed as their territory long before we arrived. One evening at dusk, I went outside to move the hose in order to water another section of our lawn. As I started to reach down to pick it up, what I thought was my hose began crawling away from me. I had mistaken a snake for the hose.

I yelled, "Honey, there's a snake here!" Gene started running around the corner of the house into the path the snake took. So I yelled, "It's coming right toward you!" Gene's high stepping was a sight to behold. But he did manage to kill the snake.

Then, one day, a huge cobra got into our workers' house. Since the snake was in a position that made it dangerous to try and kill it with a stick, Gene decided to shoot it. The blast of that gun inside those close quarters nearly deafened all of us. But he killed it, as the "scrambled snake" on the walls attested.

Sometimes we arrived home to find our dogs' eyes matted with a spitting cobra's venom. We washed out the eyes with warm milk, then treated them with antibiotic salve. The dogs recovered and were soon back to standing up to the next cobra that came along.

Tuffy, a German Shepherd who belonged to Mary Louise, killed cobras and other snakes. His method was to grab the snake behind the head, then bite and shake it until it was dead. One night he tackled an eight-foot-two-inch black mamba. It bit him before he killed it. The next morning the gardener brought Tuffy and the dead snake to us. The dog was vomiting, a sign that the venom was taking effect on his nervous system. We knew he only had a short time left unless we did something drastic.

Our son Mark had told us how to treat snakebite with electrical shock from a 12-volt battery. He had learned this from his brother-

in-law, a Wycliffe missionary in the jungles of South America.
Though we had never used this treatment, we decided the time to
try it had come. So Gene quickly rigged up the wires. He used two
pieces of insulated wires eight feet long. After stripping the insulation off each end of the wires, he connected one wire to one spark-
plug wire and the other to a metal part of the car. I started the car
and revved the motor just above idling speed, while Gene and
Kevias, the gardener, shocked Tuffy. They were supposed to put one
wire on each side of the bite, but since Tuffy's fur was so thick, we
couldn't locate the bite. So they just chose spots on different parts
of his body to apply the shock. They shocked him for three seconds,
waited 15 seconds, then repeated the process four or five times. The
dog stopped vomiting and lived several more years.

One night a few months later, we heard our dogs giving their
special snake bark. We ran outside with the flashlight. There we
found a large puff adder, with venom much like that of the rat-
tlesnake. Gene killed it while I held the light. Then we examined
our dogs and found a knot over Goldie's eye where she had been
bitten. (Goldie was a Labrador mix.) We shocked her, and the next
morning the knot was gone, with no bad effects on her.

Pythons were protected game in Zimbabwe, so we had to learn
to live with these constrictors. Outside our fence at Sasame was a
big eroded area where building rubble had been thrown. A huge
python lived in this ravine. One day while in the house, I heard a
goat bleating, "Baa-aa-aa-aa-aa." Then nothing! I ran outside to see
what was happening and found the goat in the python's vise with
the life squeezed out of it. When the snake saw me, he left the goat
and went back down in his hole. Neighborhood dogs came by and
claimed the goat as their meal. This happened four more times that
day before the snake managed to get a goat down into his "dining
room" where he could enjoy his dinner.

One night we heard our chickens making a terrible racket. The
next morning we found that two small pythons had squeezed
through the small space between the top of the bricks of the chicken
house and the corrugated asbestos roofing tiles. They had swallowed
several of our young chicks and then couldn't get back out. When
we opened the house, the remaining hens ran outside, and the
snakes, hoping for a quick escape, regurgitated their meal. The

police arrived, captured the snakes in tow sacks, and took them away. After that, our chickens refused to go back into that house. They preferred roosting outside.

Life on the mission field can be many things, but it's never boring! Even the frightening and often irritating "shadows" of God's creatures were a part of our journey. Once again, His rescue was sure.

Chapter 13

Ministry of Interruptions

"Though I am free and belong to no man, I make myself a slave to everyone, to win as many as possible . . .. I have become all things to all men so that by all possible means I might save some"
—1 Corinthians 9:19, 22.

One morning during my Quiet Time I meditated on these words in Matthew 9:36: "When he (Jesus) saw the crowds, he had compassion on them . . .." I asked myself, "Do I see people through Jesus' eyes?" I decided the answer was, "No."

As I continued to contemplate my answer, I decided, "Maybe that's why I get impatient and lack compassion for them so often." So, I prayed, "Lord, help me see people today with your eyes. I want your compassion for all I meet today."

I got up from my knees and got busy with that day's work, which was plentiful. I was particularly concerned about a writing deadline for a Sunday School lesson assignment because I was behind on it. Just as I settled down at the typewriter, I heard a knock at the door.

"I can't believe it! Another interruption!" I steamed.

Since Gene wasn't home, I trudged to the door and found a young, European man for whom we'd been praying, along with his wife. In this book I will refer to them by the pseudonyms "Larry" and "Fran."

Larry asked to see Gene. I could tell Larry was troubled. Suddenly I remembered my prayer that morning, and immediately my attitude changed. Instead of resenting his intrusion, my heart went out to him.

"Gene isn't home, but may I help you?" I said as I invited him into the house.

Over a cup of tea and some cookies, he began to tell me that his dog had been killed that morning by baboons. As I listened, he shared other burdens. He and Fran were having difficulties in their marriage and needed help. I told Larry that Jesus cared about his hurts and had the answer to his issues. Before he left, I prayed for him and Fran.

Neither were members of our church. Fran had been brought up in another church with which Larry didn't agree. At the time Larry was far from the Lord and any church. Since Larry respected Gene, he wanted Gene to counsel them.

In the ensuing weeks, as Gene talked with them, they worked out many differences, and God began to heal their troubled marriage. They started attending Bible study, and both made commitments to Jesus Christ as Lord and Savior.

* * * * *

When we moved to Gokwe, our lives were filled with interruptions from morning until night. Since we were far from town, at first we agreed as a form of ministry to sell groceries to the people who worked for us. We bought items wholesale in big quantities, and sold the items for the price we paid. This at first seemed a very charitable thing to do. The difficulty with this occurred when not only our workers but others also were almost constantly at our door wanting to buy something.

For example, as I prepared a Bible study for a lay-leaders' meeting, I'd often hear someone say, "*Go-go-go-i*" ("knock-knock"). When I arrived at the door, the person would say, "Please, madam, I want to buy shoogah (sugar)."

With as much kindness and patience as I could muster, I would finish with that customer and settle back to my work. Again, the knock arrived from someone wanting cooking oil or beans or soap. As this continued, my kindness and patience began to wear thin. This became no longer a spiritual ministry but a real bother that kept both Gene and me from the ministry to which we were called.

So we set definite hours when only our workers could buy from us. That didn't solve the problem either. Eventually we took orders from our employees once a month when we paid them. We helped them work out their lists of what they would need for the month, and they bought everything at that time.

At other times, we experienced interruptions that we welcomed. These were from people asking us to visit their village and begin a church. It was a joy to have these folks arrive, saying they wanted to receive Jesus! It was worth dropping everything to explain the way of salvation and then hear them pray the sinner's prayer, inviting Jesus into their lives.

Our area of work included almost 150 square miles, and we were situated almost in the center of it. Much drought and famine occurred in the area, and through the years, Gene was involved in many feeding programs. Pastors and lay leaders would ride the bus to talk with Gene about the need for food among their people. Some of the buses passed our way about 5 a.m. From the other direction, they arrived in the afternoon.

Gene got up at 5 a.m. and for an hour or more prayed while he walked. Then he arrived home, studied his Bible, and ate breakfast. At least once every week, and sometimes more often, some of these leaders would visit in order to talk with him at that early hour. It was difficult for him to have a consistent Quiet Time.

We prayed about how to handle this. Eventually God showed me a way to teach them and to help Gene at the same time. I was teaching a discipleship course in which I tried to show the importance of a Quiet Time. I mentioned Gene's habits and explained, "When you see my husband out early in the mornings, he is praying as he walks. This is a very important time for him when he seeks direction from the Lord."

Then I suggested, "Why not bring your Bibles when you come to talk with *M'fundisi* (missionary). Find a quiet spot, read the

Bible, and pray until about 8:00. Then come to our house, and we'll give you breakfast. Then he'll be happy to talk with you."

This worked much better, but some did not abide by our suggestions.

The interruptions that were the most difficult occurred on Sundays. Because our area was quite large, we often held weekend meetings away from our home. When we did this, we camped in our tent. People from five to 10 churches joined together for these sessions. Sometimes we went on Fridays and started the meetings that night. We continued until Sunday afternoon and concluded with a baptism and celebration of the Lord's Supper. Other times we began on Saturday. Regardless when we began, by the time we returned home late Sunday afternoon or evening—driving two or three hours to get there—we were exhausted. We just wanted a shower and a chance to relax quietly at home.

Instead of being able to rest, we usually arrived home to find lay leaders waiting at our door for us. These men always had important business to discuss with Gene, and they, of course, needed some food and a place to stay. Gene often requested that they not visit on Sundays, but some seemed to forget and visited then anyway. Sometimes we were so tired that we didn't greet them with kindness and compassion but with impatience. Exhausted, we had no more of ourselves to give.

Even during the week, co-workers arrived on business and needed a place to stay, so we eventually prepared a "prophet's room" (with bed and bath) in the workers' quarters as a place for them to stay. We arranged for our workers, who lived in the other room, to cook meals for our guests when we were too tired to do so or were too busy elsewhere. Eventually, when these visitors arrived unexpectedly on Sundays, we showed them to this room, made arrangements for their food, and told them we'd see them the next morning. Then we got our much-needed rest.

Often when I grew impatient with all those who interrupted my plans and drained my energy, God gently nudged me back to His Word and showed me how Jesus dealt with everyone. He always had compassion on them and loved them.

I learned to pray, "Lord, teach me to see the ministry in interruptions and use this irritation to make me more like Jesus."

Chapter 14

Perilous Journeys

*"When you pass through the waters, I will be with you . .
.When you walk through the fire, you will not be burned . . .. Since
you are precious and honored in my sight, and because I love you, I
will give men in exchange for you, and people in exchange for your
life"*

—Isaiah 43:2, 4.

Travel in the bush was always complicated at best. Flat tires and
other car trouble occurred regularly. When rain occurred, the potholes in the roads became basins filled with water. When we first
moved to the bush, we didn't have a four-wheel-drive vehicle, so we
often became stuck in both mud and sand. Few bridges existed in
the bush, and those either got washed out or were covered with
water during heavy rains. Between our house and the city were
rivers with no bridges. If rain occurred and a river flooded while we
were away from home, we had to wait for the river to go down
before we could proceed home.

Our first Christmas at Sasame in 1984 was one of those rainy times. Our daughter, Beth, was teaching at Sanyati Baptist High School 60 miles away, and she was home for the Christmas holidays. We planned to take Beth back to Sanyati on Christmas afternoon so we could eat dinner with other Sanyati missionaries.

We left home around 2 p.m. and became stuck in black clay about a mile from the house. By using a wench, we finally pulled ourselves out of the mud. About 20 miles from Sanyati we encountered a river where the water was four feet over the bridge. We decided to backtrack and detour onto a road that had water on it in many places. At one point, the water stretched out in front of us almost a quarter of a mile. That water was deep enough to be over the exhaust pipe but not dangerous or swift. As we studied what to do, some drunks on the road kept telling us, "Ah! No problem! Just cut off your engine and let us push you through."

Since it was becoming dark and we saw no alternative, we prayed about whether to accept the drunks' offer. Then we put ourselves in God's rescuing hands as the hilarious drunks pushed our powerless truck through the water. John and Beth got out of the truck and walked with these men, laughing and having a great adventure.

By the time we arrived in Sanyati, we had spent six hours on the road. Usually the trip took one-and-a-half to two hours. At 8 p.m., the concerned Sanyati missionaries joined us in giving praise to God for His mercy in getting us safely there. We ate our warmed-over but delicious Christmas dinner and joined in the fun and fellowship with our co-workers.

On another occasion after we moved to Sasame in 1984, Gene and I were traveling on a very slippery road when we became stuck. We were passing through a village at the time. Some of the villagers stopped their work, brought their oxen, and pulled us out of the mud. The rest of the journey, Gene gripped the steering wheel tightly and cautiously maneuvered the vehicle as it slipped and slid dangerously close to trees that grew all along the edge of the bush trail. I couldn't bear to watch that frightening scene, so I closed my eyes and sang over and over the following song that the Lord gave me:

Oh my God shall supply all our needs;
Oh my God shall supply all our needs,
According to His riches in glory by Christ Jesus;
Oh my God shall supply all our needs.

So give thanks in each circumstance;
So give thanks in each circumstance;
For He's using all things to work out for our good;
So give thanks in each circumstance.

During those difficult days when getting stuck in the mud was only one of many perils we faced, I paraphrased Habakkuk 3:17-19 like this:

Though our son is ill and his healing is a long time in coming,
Though the well fails and there is no water in our tank,
Though the rains make the roads as slippery as glass
*   and we have no four-wheel vehicle,*
Though the bugs and mosquitoes and flies become a plague
*   and fill our house,*
Yet we will rejoice in the Lord, we will be joyful
*   in God our Savior,*
The Sovereign Lord is our strength; he makes our feet
*   like the feet of a deer,*
He enables us to go on the heights.

When we finally received a four-wheel-drive vehicle, I had to learn when and how to use it. Finally, even when Gene was not with me, I was able to plow bravely through rivers, mud, and sand.

Through the years, God rescued us in all kinds of other travel mishaps, too. Once when I was taking a truckload of women to a convention in Gwelo (Gweru), we narrowly escaped an accident when the front tire on our truck blew out. Another time Gene accidentally struck and killed a donkey that ran in front of the vehicle he was using to drive a group of women to a meeting. No one in the vehicle was injured, but the radiator was cracked and the truck was out of commission for some time.

In August, 1981, while we lived in Triangle, I drove six young women to a weekend YWA (Young Women's Association) meeting in Gweru, where I was to be the guest speaker. On the way home, all the young women wanted to sit together in the back of the pickup so they could sing and discuss the things they had learned. This left me alone in the cab.

As I drove, I sang and praised the Lord. After a while, I saw a man on a bicycle pedal toward me. He wove from side to side, so I slowed down. Nearing him, I traveled very slowly, but he seemed to set his course straight at me. The following poem I wrote at the time tells what happened.

VICTORY THROUGH SORROW, 1982

My heart overflowed with love for my Lord;
My thoughts were filled with His praise
As I drove down the road on my journey home
From the meeting of YWA's.

Deep down in my mind I was also aware
Of the message I'd brought that day—
That we're in a great war with our arch enemy
And our victory will come in God's way.

But I never dreamed of the schemes Satan planned
Against six precious girls and me;
Yet there in the road, heading straight for my truck,
Came a bike as plain as could be.

I cried out, "God help," as I braked and I swerved,
But I heard a crash, and could see
A man shot through the air, through the windshield he came
And landed, face down, beside me.

No sound from his lips, no crying for help,
His spirit so quickly had fled;
What torture of mind, what grief felt my soul,
As I realized the man was dead.

The enemy's plan was to torment my thoughts
With depression, guilt, and a whine.
Yet, through day and night I heard my Lord say,
"I've called you by name, you are mine!

"Through the storms you must pass,
*   through the fire you must go,*
But I'm with you all of the way;
I'll keep you from harm, for I love you, my child.
Do not fear, just hear what I say."

To Isaiah forty-three He led me to turn,
And I knew, as His Word unfurled,
That my life He had spared, along with the girls,
Though another He'd called from this world.

And as I read on, He was saying to me
That through this event He'd win out;
Lost souls would be saved and called by His name,
Then people His praises would shout.

With my eyes full of tears, I said, "Thank you, dear Lord,
For the trial you've brought me through.
Though my heart still breaks o'er the death of a man,
I know that you cared for him, too.

So I'll trust you, my Lord, though I don't understand
Why we grow through heartache and pain;
But I know that you, too, were acquainted with grief,
And the victory is Yours once again.

The accident happened across the road from a Seventh-Day Adventist Mission. No one in the vehicle I was driving was injured. Two of the young women with me found a phone and called the police and the missionaries in Gweru. Two co-workers arrived immediately. Some of the Adventist missionaries also offered support. Thankfully, this was a remote area, so a mob didn't form to gawk at the corpse lying on the hood.

This accident occurred just over a year after Zimbabwe's independence. With Africans now in control and with a black police force, I was apprehensive about what would happen. But God took care of that potential problem by sending some very kind, compassionate, capable, fair-minded African police to investigate the case.

In the days ahead, I dealt with the guilt and despair that clung to me like a thick blanket. Eventually I was told that no charges would be filed against me. "In fact," the police said, "had the man lived, he would have been charged." The autopsy showed the man had a very high level of alcohol in his blood, and the accident marks on the road showed the man was at fault. These facts alleviated my legal guilt, but only God could heal the inner guilt and heartache.

As I yielded it all to Him and stayed in His Word, He let His light shine on my troubled heart and brought peace in my valley of deep despair.

PART 6

GOD'S FAITHFULNESS

"Because of the Lord's great love we are not consumed, for his compassions never fail. They are new every morning; great is your faithfulness"

—Lamentations 3:22-23.

Chapter 15

Reaping a Harvest

*"Let us not become weary in doing good, for at the proper time
we will reap a harvest if we do not give up"*
—Galatians 6:9.

*"Those who sow in tears will reap with songs of joy. He who
goes out weeping, carrying seed to sow,*
will return with songs of joy, carrying sheaves with him"
—Psalm 126:5-6.

Southern Baptists began working in Southern Rhodesia in 1950
with the appointment of Clyde and Hattie Dotson. The next year,
they opened the Sanyati Baptist Mission station in rural Sanyati.
With the arrival of Drs. Giles and Wana Ann Fort, a hospital was
begun. A few years later, Baptist clinics, schools, and churches were
started in the neighboring Gokwe Tribal Trust Lands.

In 1958-59, Bud Fray, while principal of the Sanyati primary
schools, ministered occasionally with Clyde Dotson in eastern
Gokwe, where Clyde lived at the time. In 1963, after Bud and his
wife Jane visited the vast Gokwe area as well as Tongaland, God

gave them a deep desire to reach this needy area for Christ. Bud's desire was to do evangelism and church planting full time. He and Jane told the Rhodesian Mission about their call, and at the end of 1963 they with their children moved into a prefab house and opened the Sasame Baptist Mission Station on the banks of the Sasame River, 60 miles from Sanyati. Next, they set up a metal hut for a clinic. Dr. Sam Cannata visited weekly from Sanyati to work in the clinic. In November, 1964, Sam and his wife Ginny with their children moved to Sasame. God blessed the evangelistic zeal and medical missions of these two couples; people were brought to a saving faith in Jesus, and churches were begun. Other faithful missionaries followed, and the Gokwe work continued to grow until 1976 when the missionaries, African pastors, and clinic staff had to leave because of the war.

When we moved to Sasame in February, 1984, we began building on the strong foundation that had been laid years before by all these servants of God. In June, Nurse Mary Louise Clark joined us at Sasame and started working with the Gokwe Clinics. Dr. Rob and Eloise Garrett, who had served at Sasame during the 1970s, also planned to join us, but because of Rob's health, they had to return to the States. The five of us had begun to bathe the work in prayer long before anyone moved to the area.

In the beginning, we felt an almost tangible presence of satanic forces around us. Each night we heard the drums beating to appease the ancestral spirits or to ask the spirits for rain. We longed to see these dear people come to know the truth and freedom in Christ. Much of the ground that had been won for the Lord in years past had been lost through communist indoctrination, persecution, and sin.

In this huge, rural northwestern area of Zimbabwe known as Gokwe, we faced a task that seemed impossible to us but not for our Lord. We knew it was His will to revive the existing churches and begin new ones.

When we arrived in 1984, one seminary-trained pastor, Jeffrey Ncube, served at a church about an hour-and-a-half drive from us. The building in which his church met was one of the few that had not been destroyed during the war. Most of the men who led the other 40 churches in the area were untrained. So we asked God to send us five seminary-trained pastors. By 1986, He had answered that request. Joining Jeffrey Ncuba were Driver Lunga, Geoffrey Gandiwa and Freedom Keri, who were farmers and lay leaders in the area before finishing their studies at the Baptist Seminary in Gweru. The fifth was Clement Chipunza, who, while working as a gardener in the Triangle area, had been saved. The Lord called him to preach under the ministries of Gene and Pastor John Neganda. We had experienced the joy of helping to disciple him and encourage him during his seminary training. Several years after he finished seminary, while serving as a pastor of a growing church in Harare, the Runyararo Baptist Church in Triangle called him as pastor. God used him greatly there.

During 1985 while we were on furlough and leave of absence, the Sasame Baptist Church on the mission station extended a call to Pastor Chipunza, and he accepted. By the time we returned to the field in June, 1986, he was at Sasame, helping to reap the rich harvest in that needy area. Though Jeffrey is now a pastor in Gweru, the other four are still faithfully serving the Lord in Gokwe, while some of their children are also now in ministry.

We praised God for each pastor He sent, and then we asked God for another five—to make 10 in all. As we had done in Triangle, we also asked Him to send us young men to disciple for Him. God answered our prayers, and by 1995 when we went on our last furlough before retirement in 1996, we had 12 seminary-trained pastors and many trained lay preachers in the Gokwe area. By the year 2001, the number of trained pastors rose to 30. Only God could do this, and He did it in several ways.

One day I heard a knock at our door. I answered it and saw a clean-cut, nice looking young man with intelligent eyes smiling at me. He held out his hand and said, "My name is Josiah. God has called me to preach, and I want to go to seminary."

We had learned from past experiences that many could claim to have a call from God in order to get financial help for an education, even if it was a seminary education. So I proceeded with caution as I shook his hand, invited him in, and summoned Gene. After talking with him, checking with the leader of his church, and praying about how best to help him, Gene and I decided to invite him to live in the workers' quarters so we could disciple him. He helped in our garden, went with us to preaching points and churches, and took discipleship courses. During the next year and a half of on-the-job training, he grew in the Lord, married a fine young lady, and then entered the Baptist seminary in Gweru. Today, Josiah Tanyarara is pastor of a church in the Gokwe area. In 2001, he finished a second course at seminary which qualifies him to teach Bible in school to supplement his income as pastor of this rural church.

Next arrived Moses Mugariri, John Makanda, Rozert Maposa, Luckson Chiombera, and many others whom we discipled, most of whom later went to seminary. In this way, God was raising up pastors for churches there.

The people were subsistence farmers, and some of the leaders took the vernacular course at the seminary in Gweru. These intensive yearly 10-week courses were taught during their less-busy season of farming. They completed the course in four years. Three of our first pastors, as well as many since then, were trained in this way. The seminary also provided a course for their wives.

The missionaries prior to us had always held an annual Layman's Bible School when the lay preachers of the whole area joined together for a week's training. Gene continued this practice, and God greatly blessed these times when pastors and missionaries taught and trained these men. Gene eventually expanded these yearly meetings to include one in the east part of the area and one in the west part.

The women were taught through WMU (Woman's Missionary Union or *Musangano weMadzimai*). Besides that, we wanted to give all the people more in-depth teaching. So we divided the area into nine districts with between five to 10 churches and preaching points in each district. We began quarterly meetings in each of the nine districts where 25 to 50 leaders—male, female and youth—would arrive for training. The trained pastors helped us teach. Those who weren't leaders also attended. We combined the daytime teaching sessions with nighttime evangelistic services when we showed the *Jesus* film and invited the whole village. God's Spirit worked in a marvelous way, and hundreds were saved.

From the beginning, we provided strong teachings on what the Bible says about the occult, spirit mediums, witch doctors, witchcraft, wearing of charms and amulets, ancestor worship, and divination as well as doctrinal, moral, ethical, stewardship, and discipleship teachings. We saturated the whole area with simple, inexpensive booklets in the vernacular that taught about these subjects. People were hungry to read and eagerly purchased these booklets for 15 to 50 cents. As God's Word filled their hearts, their lives and customs started to change. God delivered many from demons, which they called *midzimu* or ancestral spirits. They gave up their charms and spirit cloths and took a strong stand for Jesus.

These meetings were times of teaching as well as joyous spiritual fellowship. The people ate together, sang, danced, testified, and played their drums, kudu horns, and tambourines. This would have gone on all night if we hadn't suggested that they get some rest for the teaching sessions the next day. Africans have rhythm in their bones, and they did the WMU shuffle, the YWA sway, the Brotherhood boogey, the RA rumble, and the GA gait as they praised the Lord together.

Gene and I also initiated Theological Education by Extension in the area. Many leaders were so hungry to learn God's Word that some would walk or ride their bicycle two hours or more, sometimes through dangerous elephant country, to get to the classes. The men and women who led the churches grew stronger in Him as they were taught His Word.

We not only asked God for more trained pastors and leaders, we also asked God to double the 40 churches to 80 by the time we retired. God didn't do just that! When we retired, 88 churches and preaching points existed in the area. Only God could do that! He did it through ordinary people, yielded to His Spirit, and ready to share Jesus with others.

Here's an example of how many of these churches were begun: A Baptist layman who worked in one of the clinics invited Gene and Pastor Ncube to go with him to his home village where no church existed. They went, and a church was born. People from other villages visited that church, were saved, returned to their villages, and started other churches. From this one concerned layman, 15 churches were started. Mission leaders today call this a Church Planting Movement. Some think it is a new phenomenon, but we experienced a CPM years ago before the term became popularized.

We also asked the Lord for a great harvest of souls. The Holy

Spirit worked in individual hearts, and soon the harvest began, sometimes from seeds sown many years earlier. The Lord won people through one-on-one witnessing, through evangelistic crusades, and through the *Jesus* film, which we distributed in four languages.

God also gave us a harvest among the government schools of Gokwe. We were allowed to teach Scripture in several of them. However, since we needed help in this, God sent us Joseph and Denise Lugo and then Wes and Laurie Wilcox, all of whom were affiliated with the Southern Baptist Journeyman or International Service Corps (ISC) two-year program, to work with the youth and in the schools. Today Wes and Laurie are Southern Baptist career missionaries in Zambia, working with the Tonga people, one of the tribes with which they worked while with us. Joseph and Denise are now faithfully serving the Lord in the States.

Before they were baptized, those who made professions of faith had to attend a discipleship class, where they were taught Christian doctrine and what it means to be a Christian. They were not baptized until they renounced all their pagan practices. Between 1984 and October, 1995, the fewest Gene and our pastors baptized in one year was 250; the most was 817.

Gene baptized 164 on one Sunday in one place. That time he baptized in a pool where elephants had been trampling, but this was not the usual location for baptisms. We didn't have church buildings or regular baptismal pools. Because of the risk of bilharzia from the pools and streams and since there was very little water in most places, Gene devised his own way to baptize. The men would dig a grave-like hole in the ground six-and-one-half-feet long, four-feet wide, and two-feet deep. With plastic sheets in the "pool," three drums of water gave us 18 inches of water. The candidate would sit on the bottom of the pool with his or her feet stretched out, while Gene knelt beside him or her. When Gene immersed the person, he or she was lying on the bottom of the pool.

A layman from a new preaching point arrived one day to tell Gene that their group had 17 people ready for baptism. He mentioned the lack of water in the area and asked my husband what they were to do. Gene told him about digging the hole and gave him some plastic for it. Then they talked about other things. Before he left, he said, "Now tell me again about that hole."

Since he had been baptized in a church pool, the man didn't understand. So Gene said, "Dig it like you dig a grave." The man left, and Gene didn't see him again until the Sunday of the baptism. On arrival, Gene found that the man had done exactly as he had been told. The hole was six-feet deep with 18 inches of water in it. During the baptism, the people couldn't see the candidates or Gene. But when they came crawling out of that grave, it truly pictured resurrection! It was one of the most meaningful baptismal services he's ever led. It illustrated that the candidates had truly died with Christ to sin, been buried with Him, and then raised with Him to live a new life through His power.

In another place, Gene had to baptize 57 people. While church members were filling the pool with water from a borehole, the well went dry and they only had a foot of water in the pool. The people asked Gene, "What are we going to do, M'fundisi (Missionary)?

"We're going to baptize," answered Gene.

As he baptized the people, each of them took some of the water out in their clothes. By the time he put number 57 under, the person's nose was sticking out of the water. So Gene turned the person's head to the side and finished the immersion.

Gene and I also prayed about another need in the area. We asked God for 25 church buildings. We had observed that the congregations that had buildings remained stronger than those that didn't have buildings. Most groups met under trees or in pole shelters with thatched roofs. Meeting in either of these, the people were at the mercy of the weather. The hot sun would stream in or the rain would pour through the thatch. Some were plastered with mud, but in a few years, the termites would destroy them and the people had to rebuild. If they met in homes, clannishness often developed. The church became known as belonging to the one in whose village it met. A few groups met in school classrooms. But the time often came when they were asked to move out of the school.

Many of the church buildings had been destroyed during the war, and the people couldn't afford to rebuild. So when they visited us with requests for buildings, we, by faith, told them, "If you will make the mud bricks, burn them, haul the sand and water, and do all the work, we will furnish the cement, window and door frames, and the tin roof.

By the time we were ready to retire, God had given us more than we asked for. These dear people had built 33 simple church buildings. Since our retirement, they have built others. These are not large, nor elegant, but small, simple places of worship that stand as a witness in the heathen community that Jesus is Lord. Also, the members take pride in these.

Because so many adults in the area couldn't read, God led me to train the leaders to teach adult literacy. Then they began literacy classes in their villages. I started teaching my neighbors in the Tsivi village to read. The husband and father of the village was a tribal headman who had five wives. He was a very kind, helpful neighbor, but he was lost, steeped in paganism and ancestor worship.

Nurse Mary Louise had a tremendous caring ministry to the mothers of the under-five babies and children. For some time, she had been caring for the sick five-year-old daughter of the village father, *Baba* (translated father, mister) Tsivi. Finally the child died, and Mary Louise, along with other missionaries and church members, ministered to the family and showed them Christ's love.

The following Sunday, *Baba* and one of his wives attended church and responded at the invitation. He gave his heart and life completely to the Lord Jesus and became like a new person. As soon as *Baba* Tsivi was saved, we began to notice a difference in the night sounds. The drums that had beat in the night for so many years to appease the ancestral spirits and those that beat to accompany their orgies of beer drinking were now silent. In a short while, we started hearing a new drumbeat. We would hear chorus singing and praise songs to the Lord accompanied by their "converted" drums. *Baba* Tsivi's son, who was already saved, would read the Bible to him each night. This son gave testimony to his father's faithfulness to Christ when his friends tried to get him to go back to the old ways.

I combined the literacy classes in the village with Bible studies. What joy a year later to have several of these formerly illiterate ladies stand up in church and read from the Bible. Then one of them introduced a woman she was teaching to read. One by one, several of the Tsivi wives came to the Lord along with several of his children and daughters-in-law. It was a unique experience to disciple a polygamous family, but it helped me see how great is God's grace.

Our churches accepted polygamous believers as members, but these members were not allowed to hold any office, and the men were disciplined if they took additional wives. The churches were very firm in teaching that God's plan for marriage was one husband and one wife "till death do you part."

In 1996, *Baba* Tsivi died. He was a strong witness to the end. Then in 1998, his daughter who had been one of my best students in the literacy class died of AIDS. Her unsaved husband had been unfaithful to her for years. I had often cried and prayed with her for his salvation. He had died of AIDS a few months before she went to be with the Lord, leaving three orphans. Though sad over these deaths, we rejoice that she and her father are now with Jesus.

Another ministry God gave us that helped to reap a harvest was in the field of hunger and relief. This part of the country had many droughts. Being subsistence farmers, the people lived from one growing season to the next. If their crops failed, they went hungry. Thanks to Southern Baptists' gifts to hunger and relief, many thousands were kept alive physically, and hundreds of these people were saved spiritually. In our region, Baptists were known as "the people who care" because of the loving concern and help we provided.

As we got ready to leave for our last furlough in 1995, another famine occurred. We thought, "We just don't have time to carry on another feeding program." Then we prayed, "Lord, what are we to do?"

One day one of the nurses from the clinic told us that one of our church members was very sick. We recognized his illness as starvation. We then put in a request to the Mission Board for a volunteer to help with a feeding program. This request was answered through our youngest son, Paul, and his wife Shana. Paul received his bachelor of arts degree in psychology from Gardner Webb College. Then he graduated in 1992 from Southwestern Baptist Theological Seminary in the field of communications. Today, he works fulltime as a video editor for FamilyNet, a program of the North American Mission Board, and also does some freelance videography through his company, PLP Productions. When he and Shana heard about our need, they volunteered to help. They spent three months carrying on this relief project, as well as helping us pack, sell, or give away the accumulations of 39 years.

Paul and his siblings, along with their mates and children, produced a video for our farewell at the annual Zimbabwe Baptist Mission meeting in 1995. Each of our children assured us that growing up on the mission field was a great blessing to them, and they thanked us for giving them this privilege.

As our precious African friends gathered to tell us goodbye before we left, many tears were shed. Through these tears, we praised God for His faithfulness in doing the impossible in this land where He had planted us for all these years. And we knew that His faithfulness would continue into the next phase of our journey.

PART 7

UNTIL HE COMPLETES THE JOURNEY

God, I want to be like Jesus;
Through me may His light shine.
But I fail in ways unnumbered
To be like your Son divine.

So, Lord, put me in your furnace,
But in the flames please stay with me,
In your love, keep on refining,
Till your image shines in me.
                                        —Jean Phillips

" . . . *Forgetting what is behind and straining toward what is*
ahead, I press on toward the goal to win the prize for which God
has called me heavenward in Christ Jesus . . . who . . .will trans-
form our lowly bodies so that they will be like his glorious body"
                          —Philippians 3:13-14, 21.

Chapter 16

Trial by Fire

"For you, O God, tested us; you refined us like silver . . . we went through fire . . . but you brought us to a place of abundance."
　　　　　　　　　　　　—Psalm 66:10-12.

"These have come so that your faith of greater worth than gold . . . may be proved genuine . . . "
　　　　　　　　　　　　—1 Peter1:7.

"Guard my life and rescue me; let me not be put to shame, for I take refuge in you."
　　　　　　　　　　　　—Psalm 25:20.

On the night we were abducted in 1999, our son Mark received a phone call at his home in Columbia, SC, telling him what had happened to us. Janice, his wife, immediately phoned her mother, Joy, a retired missionary to Venezuela. Joy began praying for us and for the thieves. She prayed, "Lord, make that car troublesome to them so they'll know they are sinning against you in stealing it."

God answered that prayer in a dramatic way. On the afternoon of the day we were kidnapped, the thieves were driving our car in the high mountains of Lesotho quite a distance north of where they left us. When rounding a sharp bend in the road, they went into a ditch and bent the wheels so badly that they couldn't move the vehicle. The police arrived, and an officer arrested the driver when he saw that the car had no license plate. (The thieves had apparently removed it.) Because communication in Lesotho is very slow, the police hadn't heard of our abduction, so they let the other men go. But they kept the driver in order to investigate the unlicensed vehicle.

Missionary Charles Middleton had planned a leadership training meeting for the pastors and lay leaders in the Lesotho churches. It was to be held that same day at Katse, in the vicinity of the kidnappers' accident. After he knew we were OK, Charles went ahead with his plans.

Two of the leaders traveled to the meeting on a bus that had to pass along the same road the thieves had traveled. These young leaders had been working with us in Thabana Mohlomi. One of them, Leseli, had been in our vehicle the day before the abduction. The bus they were riding suddenly stopped. They looked out the window to see a vehicle partially blocking the road. Leseli and the other man quickly realized it was not just any vehicle, but it was our Venture. The recognition was confirmed when Leseli saw the folding chairs he had packed still in the back of the car.

The bus continued on its journey to Katse. There, the young men reported to Charles what they had seen. Charles then contacted the police. Meanwhile, back at the police station, the officer in charge was preparing to release the driver but halted that process when Charles told him about the abduction and theft of the vehicle. Charles identified the car and located the car's papers, which were still in the glove compartment and made out in the name of the Baptist Mission in South Africa.

It was too late in the evening for Charles to tow the vehicle away. So he went back the next day to do this. By then, thieves had stripped the vehicle of everything of value. Nothing was left but the bare shell.

God used the accident to answer Joy's prayer. As a direct result of the accident, four men involved in the abduction were eventually arrested. (Ironically, it was never clear to us exactly how many were involved in the abduction. Gene saw five; I saw only four. We do agree that four were in the car when they freed us.) We do not know if any of the men have ever admitted to the Lord that they sinned against Him, not just in this, but in falling short of His glory. (See Romans 3:23.) But we continue to pray for them, and have asked hundreds of others to join us in asking God to bring them to repentance and salvation in Jesus. We ask you, as readers of this book, to join us in this prayer.

After the trauma of the abduction, God began to heal our memories. (See Psalm 107:20.) Nevertheless, we put in place a security system in the form of reinforced burglar bars on all windows and the door. We also hired a night guard and secured a guard dog, Laurie, from the Middletons. We put up a fence around our house and had beepers that made a loud noise when activated. Without electricity, that was about the best we could do.

Because of his protective nature, Gene experienced more fear and caution afterwards than I did. As for me, I slept well and wasn't afraid, even after two of the thieves were released on bail. Tseou, our neighbor, told us he knew these youths and felt sure they had been led astray by the others.

But my state of mind changed significantly in mid-May when the last two of our abductors, the more hardened criminals, were released from prison on bail. Our neighbors told us about seeing the thieves in Morija. Several times we heard friends say, "They were actually bragging about their crime."

Because of the darkness the night they kidnapped us, neither Gene nor I knew what the men looked like. Consequently, I found myself looking suspiciously at any stranger I met. I'd think, "Could this be one of them?"

Some threats were made against the life of Peete, our guard, because he worked for us. He had gone to school with two of the thieves. We sensed at times that he seemed to be anxious. He said he was happy in his work and wanted to stay with us. We prayed with him and encouraged him in his newfound faith.

One day Gene and I arrived home from a meeting and were driving up the mountain to our cottage. On the side of the road was a man lying very still. Gathered around him were several people. They told us that he had raped an old African woman who lived higher up on the side of the mountain. The neighbors had done instant "African justice" by catching him and almost beating him to death.

This was a vivid reminder of the fact that rape was a real possibility. Satan began to play tricks on my mind. Our cottage had open rafters, a tin roof, and a ceiling up next to the roof. Some creature must have gotten into the narrow space between the roof and the ceiling, because I began hearing scratching sounds. The roof also creaked and groaned at night, giving out sounds I had been sleeping through. But now these sounds woke Gene and me. We told ourselves it was nothing, committed ourselves to the Lord, and went back to sleep.

But Sunday night, May 30, was different. That evening, when Peete came to work, he mentioned having seen our abductors that afternoon. They were drinking and smoking marijuana. He also told us that the toothache he had been battling for a week was worse. He also had a headache and was on pain medication. Monday morning he was to have oral surgery and would not be able to work for the next several nights.

When Gene and I went to bed, all the things Peete had told us began to work on our thoughts. A full moon was in the sky this night just as it had been on the night we were abducted. The creature in the ceiling was making noises that sounded like someone sawing through the burglar bars. Peete was very quiet, and we didn't see him making his usual rounds. I thought, "Peete's medication has put him to sleep." Then I reasoned, "It's alright. If anyone were out there, the dog would bark." But the idea popped into my head, "She can't bark if she's been killed." Satan was torturing my mind by filling me with fear. Finally, we saw the glow of Peete's flashlight as he passed our window on his rounds. After a while we fitfully slept.

The next morning we were exhausted. We realized our scars were deeper than we suspected. We acknowledged the truth: we needed counseling. Now was the time to obtain it, since the right counselor had just arrived in Johannesburg. Jeff Fray, son of missionaries Bud and Jane Fray, who had kept our son John in

Johannesburg years earlier, had sold his practice in Knoxville, TN, and was now a missionary and counselor in our area. Jeff had grown up with our children in Zimbabwe. He and his wife had arrived as International Service Corps (ISC) volunteers to conduct pastoral counseling with hurting missionaries. We were definitely hurting, and this godly, well-qualified psychologist was the right man to help us.

We phoned Charles and asked him to make an appointment for us with Jeff. Since we wouldn't have a guard for several nights, the Middletons invited us to spend that time with them. After packing and arranging for our neighbor to feed the dog, we left home around 5:15 p.m. for what should have been a 45-minute trip.

On our way down the mountain, a young man to whom we had witnessed stopped us to ask for a ride of a short distance. Conscious of the need to get to our destination before the winter darkness set in, we nevertheless took time to talk with him as he rode with us. Because travel in Lesotho is so hazardous, we tried not to travel after dark. Since traffic was quite heavy that afternoon, we were still five or 10 minutes from the Middletons' house when darkness descended upon us.

Suddenly, in the light of an oncoming car, I saw two men crossing the road from the right. With horror I thought, "That car is about to hit those men." Just as the car passed us, Gene and I both saw the men in the middle of the road.

Gene braked and swerved to the left, but one of the men kept walking right into our car. Quite possibly, the man behind him, trying to get out of the way of the oncoming traffic, pushed him into us. We heard a bump as he hit the mirror and wind-visor on the driver's side. Gene stopped and pulled off the road. Since 911 service is nonexistent in Lesotho, I dialed the Middletons on our cell phone.

We could see the man lying in the road, but we believed that we did not dare get out of the car because of what had happened to other people in similar situations. The previous year on this same road, three African men in a pick-up had hit and killed a high school student. When they got out of their vehicle to render assistance, a hostile crowd killed all three men.

I told the Middletons what had happened, and Charles left home immediately to join us. When a crowd began to gather and started beating on our car, we feared for our lives. So, we decided to go straight to the police station. We phoned Charles again and told him to meet us there.

With a taxi chasing us, Gene dodged in and out of traffic on our way to the police station while I prayed. Finally about halfway to the police station, the taxi rammed us, trying to force us to stop. Gene kept driving, and the taxi driver, who probably did not want to further damage his car, quit the chase.

The trauma of the accident, plus the frightening chase, unnerved us to such a degree that by the time we reached the police station, we were both shaking so hard we could hardly talk. As Gene began telling the police about the accident, Charles arrived.

After explaining what happened and why we left, several policemen went with us back to the scene of the accident. The crowd had dispersed. We learned that since no ambulances are available, a taxi had taken the man to the hospital where he had been pronounced dead.

When the police finally finished with us and let us go home with Charles, we were totally exhausted. Gene was more devastated than I had ever seen him. My sensitive, caring husband was weighed down with the burden of the man's death. Neither of us slept much that night.

The next morning, Gene and Charles returned with the police to the scene of the accident so they could record all the road markings in the daylight. Charles also took pictures of the road and of our car to show the broken side mirror and wind guard on the driver's side. The picture showed the dent on our right fender the taxi made when the driver was trying to stop us. The color of the taxi's paint was highly visible in the dent.

Later that morning, Gene had to appear before the magistrate, where he was charged with culpable homicide. He had to post R300.00 bond (US$50.00). A hearing was set for June 15. Charles had notified the American Embassy, and its representative was with Gene during all the proceedings. The court wanted to take Gene's passport to make sure he stayed in the country. But Charles told of our recent abduction and of our scheduled appointment with the counselor on Friday in Johannesburg. After the embassy spokesperson stood good for our return, the court let Gene keep his passport.

While Gene and Charles were taking care of all the legal matters, I stayed with Charles' wife, Rebecca, at their home. I was numb, unable to pray or to concentrate on the Word. The only thing I could do was rest in the Lord's arms and let Him hold me. Rebecca helped by just being there and sharing some of the details of the death of Charles' first wife, Glenda. A few years before, while driving to a prayer retreat in South Africa, with Charles following in another vehicle, his first wife was involved in an accident and was killed. Rebecca and her first husband had served with the Middletons in Malawi. Since he had died of leukemia several years earlier, she comforted Charles in his sorrow. Later the two of them married. Because of their pasts, they could truly empathize with us in our pain in the present situation.

Just before Gene and Charles returned home for lunch, our daughter Beth and her family arrived at the Middletons' to express to us their love and comfort. Our precious grandchildren lifted my spirits and brought sunshine back into my life so I could give strength to my hurting husband.

That afternoon Charles helped Gene find a lawyer who told them, "Don't expect the trial to take place on the 15th as scheduled. From my experience, it never does. The delays usually go on and on." When told that we were booked on a flight to the States in just over two months, he said, "I'll try by all means to get the case settled before then."

The next day Charles took us to Morija, where Wes met us and helped pack our personal things. He took our belongings and us to their home in Roma. We stayed there until Friday. We continued to pack. That brought more grief because we didn't feel our work in Lesotho was finished.

With my heart breaking, I remarked, "What hurts so very much is that it seems our work in Lesotho has come to an end and the devil has won this victory."

With great assurance, Gene replied, "He may have won this battle, but he hasn't won the war."

Charles and Rebecca took us to Johannesburg on Friday for our appointment with Jeff, our counselor. He told us to consider ourselves in the hospital for a while as God healed our emotions and memories. We stayed in one of the medical apartments at Baptist

International Mission Services (BIMS), which Southern Baptists make available to sick and hurting missionaries in that part of the world.

It was much more difficult for us to snap back this time than it had been after our abduction. We had deep wounds, not only from the accident, but also from the previous traumatic incident. Yet, out of the many emotions we felt, we did not feel sorry for ourselves. One of the most difficult issues this time was the uncertainty of what the court would decide. Besides the terrible ache in our hearts caused by the man's death, Gene had a real fear that the worst might happen—that he would be sentenced to jail and his passport taken from him. Truly we needed the Lord's intervention and healing.

One day Jeff counseled Gene and me separately. He asked me to set in place a sort of mental TV screen as he walked me back through the trauma of the accident. Then he asked me where Jesus was in it all. This highly trained professional man of God gave no suggestions but let the Lord give me the pictures. I saw Jesus, not Gene, in the driver's seat, applying the brakes and swerving. I also saw Jesus standing with that man in the middle of the road, probably trying to hold him back. Next, I saw my Lord kneeling over the body as it lay in the road after the man was struck. At the same time, I felt his arms around Gene and me in the car, holding us as we cried.

This counseling session was a painful yet very precious time. By faith we had known the Lord was with us, but that day in my mind, I could more clearly see Him there. This reinforced the truth that God loved and cared for us. Though He does not cause such tragedies, God is in control whenever one of His children is involved.

Before we flew to Lesotho on Friday, June 12, some of the other missionaries lovingly prayed for us and for the outcome of the hearing. Many other friends and relatives emailed us to assure us of their prayers and to give us verses of encouragement. A number of them claimed for us God's Word in Isaiah 54:17, "no weapon forged against you will prevail, and you will refute every tongue that accuses you. This is the heritage of the servants of the Lord, and this is their vindication from me . . . " We were blessed to have Christians in many parts of the world praying for us once again.

Beth, Wes, and our grandchildren met us at the airport and drove us to their house. There we began packing our trunks for our return to the States. Lesotho winters are quite cold, but the houses there have no central heat. Nevertheless, we were grateful for another chance to be with family.

Sunday we went to Thabana Mohlomi to worship one last time. Some 100 of those precious people—counting all the children and babies—filled our little meeting place and sang praises to God. It was thrilling to hear six of these new believers quote perfectly the seven salvation verses we had encouraged them to memorize! With joy we gave each of these a Sesotho Bible. We challenged the others to continue working on the verses. We left other Bibles with their leaders to give these believers when they completed their assignment.

Gene preached for his final time there. We affirmed that what God had begun, He would bring to completion. We acknowledged "Jesus is Lord!" Then the people shouted together, "*Jesu ke Morena!*" The devil and all his demons heard their proclamation that Jesus is Lord. We closed our part of the service by urging them to let Jesus be Lord of their whole lives.

Afterwards, the women came with their loving, farewell gifts. Many of them wept. Then everyone encircled us and prayed for us audibly at the same time, as is their custom. We felt the love of Jesus flow to us through them, and our tears mingled with theirs.

On Monday, Mampho Makosholo, our dear friend, constant companion, co-laborer, and interpreter throughout our months in Lesotho, arrived in Roma to see us and to close out our work together. We wept as we talked and prayed together, committing each other into God's care. She wrote down the names of 12 people who had received Christ and wanted to be baptized and become members of the Thabana Muhlomi Baptist Church. When the weather warmed up, these were baptized. Today a small church building is situated on the land that was given by the local chief, who also accepted Christ.

We had wanted to do so much more, but after talking with Mampho, we had peace about leaving. We believed the reason God sent us to Lesotho had been accomplished. Though the harvest in that country is much slower in arriving than in Zimbabwe, we know each soul is precious to the Lord.

Wes took us to Morija on Thursday, where we visited our dear friends there again, encouraged them in the Lord, and said more tearful goodbyes. This visit gave closure to that chapter of our lives also.

As predicted, Gene's hearing was delayed until 8:30 a.m. Friday, June 18. Through email, our prayer warriors were kept aware of what was occurring. Special prayer was requested for us on the International Mission Board Prayer Line, on Christian radio station WMHK in Columbia, SC, in Baptist state papers, and through many local church prayer lines. The day before the hearing, our friends at First Baptist Church of Camden, SC, held a 24-hour prayer vigil for us. Secular television stations in Columbia and our local newspaper in Camden ran stories about our situation. This caused many more believers to pray for us. Those prayers sustained us through the delays. They also helped speed up the legal process-es. God performed a miracle by causing the trial to take place only three days later than first scheduled.

The hearing was not easy for either of us. Gene was found guilty of negligence and was sentenced to a fine of R200.00 (US\$32.00) or 12 months in jail. These were both suspended. The court let him go without paying the fine or spending time in prison. We were very happy that the case was over and that Gene was free to leave the country. Now we could return to Johannesburg and con-tinue the counseling.

Throughout this latest trauma, our concern had been for the family of the man who died. Gene met some of the family members on the day after the accident. They were wonderful and understand-ing. They suspected that their son had been to a party where he had been drinking. In accordance with Basotho custom, we gave them a substantial gift to help with the funeral and to offer our condo-lences. After everything was over, we wrote the family a letter from Johannesburg, telling of our sorrow for them and giving our testi-mony as well as sharing verses God had used to sustain and comfort us. The last part of that letter follows:

"... *Dear friends, let our Lord give you comfort, peace, and joy also. He loves you. He loved that dear one who died . . .. Jesus . . . died for us all . . . so that we might have everlasting life. But each of us must personally repent of our sins and put our faith in Jesus as the only way of salvation . . .. We must open our hearts to Jesus as He knocks at the door of our lives. We must invite Him in and receive Him so He can be Lord of our life. If any of you has never done this before, we hope you will do so now. Just pray, "Lord Jesus, I am a sinner. I cannot save myself. I believe you died for me and rose again. I repent of my sins and forsake them. I receive you now into my life. Come into my heart and make me a new person. I give you my life to control as my Lord and Master. Thank you for saving me and making me God's child. Amen."*

In closing, we wrote, *"If some of you will receive Jesus and be saved, then God can take this terrible accident and bring life out of it."*

Someone asked us, "Knowing all you know now after all that's happened, would you still have gone to Lesotho? And would you still have stayed there after your abduction?"

After thinking for a moment, I answered, "Yes, to both questions. You see, souls were saved and seeds planted through both our ordeals. We trust God to continue to reap a harvest in Lesotho."

Before we left for Lesotho, I chose to call our newsletter *Gene and Jean's Joyful Journeys*. We chose as our verse Isaiah 55:12, "You will go out with joy and be led forth in peace . . .." In the last issue before we left Johannesburg for the States, I wrote, "We believe we have been in God's will in being here and know that Romans 8:28-29 is true. These journeys have been joyful because they have been made in obedience to our Lord."

God continues to use our experiences for His glory. Though we wouldn't have chosen this way for Him to be glorified, that's what we want—His glory. When we arrived at the airport in Columbia, a large crowd of our friends from First Baptist Church of Camden, SC, along with television cameras and crew, met us. In one of the news accounts, the TV reporter told of the prayer vigil for us and showed the beautiful steeple of the church where inside believers were gathered to pray for us. Our return, the reporter said, was living proof that God answers prayer.

Now we continue our journey, knowing that God is still teaching us—and still rescuing us. And we're still ready to go wherever He leads. We're grateful that daughter Beth, her husband Wes, and our grandchildren, Jordan, Bethany, and Michelle, are today planting seeds of the gospel in Lesotho under the guidance of the International Mission Board.

At this point, I ask you, as a reader of this book, to examine your own heart and ask whether you have ever committed your life to Jesus Christ as Lord and Savior. If not, I urge you to pray the prayer suggested in the letter to the family of the man who was killed in the accident. If you do this, please contact a nearby pastor or church-staff member for guidance about future steps. Jesus is available to rescue you from sin and death and to offer you eternal life. I urge you to take Him by His outstretched hand and receive His promise of eternal life.

Chapter 17

Pressing On

"For this God is our God for ever and ever; he will be our guide even to the end"
—Psalm 48:14.

When we faced sickness, trials, and challenges, I often asked, "Why?" I imagine that all of us have asked that one-word question at some time. The psalmist also asked this question.

Through the years, I went through my Bible and marked verses about trials. I found a real pattern developing in my life. I discovered that when I encountered challenges, they made me more dependent on the Lord. He grew me during those times in ways I didn't grow when all seemed to be smooth sailing. This truth is borne out in nature. A pearl is formed under great stress. Trees grow strong when winds beat on them.

God is training His children to reign with Him. He doesn't want cowards or those who will quit the race at the first sign of fatigue. His training ground is over high hills and down into deep valleys. We go through the flood and the fire as He refines us. In order to defeat our enemy Satan, we must not "kick against the pricks." We mustn't complain but learn to rejoice in each step of God's training ground. His goal is to develop us to be more like Jesus.

Real victory over trials is not "grin and bear it." When I read about the three Hebrews in the fiery furnace and Daniel in the lions' den, I saw something that helped me understand my situation. God can take us through the fire of afflictions so we can emerge without smelling like smoke. He can bring us from the den of the lions of evil so there's no wound on us, if we continue to trust in Him. (See Dan. 3:27 and 6:23.) That's victory!

Read some of the reasons God allows trials and afflictions to occur in His children. Keep your eyes open for others as you read the Word. Then join me in saying, "Lord, whatever it takes, make me more like Jesus. Let your light shine in and through me no matter what my circumstances. And keep me faithful until the end of my journey."

WHY TRIALS AND AFFLICTIONS?

Because we live in earthly bodies in a sinful world:

" . . . In this world you will have trouble. But take heart! I have overcome the world" (John 16:33).

"I consider that our present sufferings are not worth comparing with the glory that will be revealed in us . . . For the creation was subjected to frustration, not by its own choice, but by the will of the one who subjected it, in hope that the creation itself will be liberated from its bondage to decay and brought into the glorious freedom of the children of God. We know that the whole creation has been groaning . . . Not only so, but we ourselves . . . groan inwardly as we wait eagerly for our adoption as sons, the redemption of our bodies" (Rom. 8:18-23).

"But we have this treasure in jars of clay to show that this all-surpassing power is from God and not from us. We are hard pressed on every side, but not crushed; perplexed, but not in despair; persecuted, but not abandoned; struck down, but not destroyed. We always carry around in our body the death of Jesus, so that the life of Jesus may also be revealed in our body" (2 Cor. 4:7-10).

To give us an eternal perspective:

"For our light and momentary troubles are achieving for us an eternal glory that far outweighs them all. So we fix our eyes not on what is seen, but on what is unseen. For what is seen is temporary, but what is unseen is eternal" (2 Cor. 4:17-18).

To teach us not to rely on ourselves but on God:

"We do not want you to be uninformed, brothers, about the hardships we suffered . . . We were under great pressure, far beyond our ability to endure, so that we despaired even of life. Indeed, in our hearts we felt the sentence of death. But this happened that we might not rely on ourselves but on God, who raises the dead" (2 Cor. 1:8-9).

To teach us how weak we are and how strong Christ is:

"But he said to me, 'My grace is sufficient for you, for my power is made perfect in weakness.' Therefore I will boast all the more gladly about my weaknesses, so that Christ's power may rest on me. This is why, for Christ's sake, I delight in weaknesses, in insults, in hardships, in persecutions, in difficulties. For when I am weak, then I am strong" (2 Cor. 12:9-10).

To humble us or to keep us humble:

"To keep me from becoming conceited because of these sur-passingly great revelations, there was given me a thorn in my flesh, a messenger of Satan, to torment me" (2 Cor. 12:7).

"Remember how the Lord your God led you all the way in the desert these forty years, to humble you and to test you in order to know what was in your heart . . . He humbled you, causing you to hunger and then feeding you with manna . . . to teach you that man does not live on bread alone but on every word that comes from the mouth of the Lord" (Deut. 8:2-3).

To allow us to fellowship in Christ's sufferings and become like Him:

"I want to know Christ and the power of his resurrection and the fellowship of sharing in his sufferings, becoming like him in his death" (Phil. 3:10).

"Dear friends, do not be surprised at the painful trial you are suffering, as though something strange were happening to you. But rejoice that you participate in the sufferings of Christ, so that you may be overjoyed when his glory is revealed" (1 Pet. 4:12-13).

To allow us to share in Christ's glory:

"Now if we are children, then we are heirs—heirs of God and co-heirs with Christ, if indeed we share in his sufferings in order that we may also share in his glory" Rom. 8:17.

To train us to reign with Jesus :

"If we suffer, we shall also reign with him . . . " 2 Tim. 2:12 (KJV).

To discipline and train us as God's children:

"Endure hardship as discipline; God is treating you as sons. For what son is not disciplined by his father?" "No discipline seems pleasant at the time, but painful. Later on, however, it produces a harvest of righteousness and peace for those who have been trained by it" (Heb. 12:7, 11).

"My son, do not despise the lord's discipline and do not resent his rebuke, because the lord disciplines those he loves, as a father the son he delights in" (Prov. 3:11-12).

"Those whom I love I rebuke and discipline. So be earnest, and repent" (Rev. 3:19).

To teach us to obey:

"Before I was afflicted I went astray, but now I obey your word" (Ps. 119:67).

"My ears had heard of you but now my eyes have seen you. Therefore I despise myself and repent in dust and ashes" (Job 42:5-6).

To help us develop patience and perseverance:

" . . . we glory in tribulations also: knowing that tribulation worketh patience;" (Rom. 5:3 KJV).

"My brethren, count it all joy when you fall into various trials, knowing that the testing of your faith produces patience" (Jas. 1:2-3 NKJV).

"Remember those earlier days after you had received the light, when you stood your ground in a great contest in the face of suffering. Sometimes you were publicly exposed to insult and persecution . . . You . . . joyfully accepted the confiscation of your property, because you knew that you yourselves had better and lasting possessions . . .. You need to persevere so that when you have done the will of God, you will receive what he has promised" (Heb. 10:32-36).

To allow us to share in God's holiness:

" . . . God disciplines us for our good, that we may share in his holiness" (Heb. 12:10).

To enable us to bear more fruit for him:

" . . . and every branch that bears fruit He prunes, that it may bear more fruit" (John 15:2 NKJV).

To give opportunity for our faith in God to grow:

"So then, those who suffer according to God's will should commit themselves to their faithful Creator and continue to do good" (1 Pet. 4:19).

"Blessed is the man who perseveres under trial, because when he has stood the test, he will receive the crown of life that God has promised to those who love him" (Jas. 1:12).

To give opportunity for us to comfort others:

"Praise be to the God . . . of all comfort, who comforts us in all our troubles, so that we can comfort those in any trouble . . . For just as the sufferings of Christ flow over into our lives, so also through Christ our comfort overflows" (2 Cor. 1:3-5).

To give opportunity for victory over sin:

" . . . he who has suffered in his body is done with sin. As a result, he does not live the rest of his earthly life for evil human desires, but rather for the will of God" (1 Pet. 4:1-2).

To allow others to pray for us and watch God work:

"He has delivered us from such a deadly peril, and he will deliver us. On him we have set our hope that he will continue to deliver us, as you help us by your prayers Then many will give thanks on our behalf for the gracious favor granted us in answer to the prayers of many." (2 Cor. 1:10-11).

To teach us to delight in God's Word:

"It was good for me to be afflicted so that I might learn your decrees" (Ps. 119:71).

"If your law had not been my delight, I would have perished in my affliction" (Ps. 119:92).

To prove our loyalty to God and defeat Satan:

" . . . For the accuser of our brothers, who accuses them before our God day and night, has been hurled down. They overcame him by the blood of the Lamb and by the word of their testimony; they did not love their lives so much as to shrink from death" (Rev. 12:10-11).

See also Job 1:8-12, 20-22; 2:3-10.

To bring glory to God:

"These (trials) have come so that your faith—of greater worth than gold, which perishes even though refined by fire—may be proved genuine and may result in praise, glory and honor when Jesus Christ is revealed" (1 Pet. 1:7).

To mature us:

"Perseverance must finish its work so that you may be mature and complete, not lacking anything" (Jas. 1: 4).

To refine us:

"But he knows the way that I take; when he has tested me, I will come forth as gold" (Job 23:10).

"See, I have refined you, though not as silver; I have tested you in the furnace of affliction. For my own sake, for my own sake I do this" (Is. 48:10).

To give us a platform of witness

"He lifted me out of the slimy pit, out of the mud and mire; he set my feet on a rock and gave me a firm place to stand. He put a new song in my mouth, a hymn of praise to our God. Many will see and fear and put their trust in the Lord" (Ps. 40:2-3).

"I will declare your name to my brothers; in the congregation I will praise you." "For he has not despised or disdained the suffering of the afflicted one; he has . . . listened to his cry for help" (Ps. 22:22, 24).

To give God an opportunity to deliver and show His glory:

" . . . This sickness will not end in death. No, it is for God's glory so that God's Son may be glorified through it" (John 11:4).

" . . . 'Rabbi, who sinned, this man or his parents, that he was born blind?' 'Neither this man nor his parents sinned,' said Jesus, 'but this happened so that the works of God might be displayed in his life'" (John 9:2-3).

"A righteous man may have many troubles, but the Lord delivers him from them all" (Ps. 34:19).

To prove God's love and faithfulness to us:

"Who shall separate us from the love of Christ? Shall trouble or hardship or persecution or famine or nakedness or danger or sword?" "For I am convinced that neither death nor life, neither angels nor demons, neither the present nor the future, nor any powers, neither height nor depth, nor anything else in all creation, will be able to separate us from the love of God that is in Christ Jesus our Lord" (Rom. 8:35, 38-39).

* * * * *

In closing, I'll summarize in verse the message of this book. Will you pray the last two verses with Gene and me?

Long years have passed since we began our journey.
It led us through deep sorrow, joy, and pain.

But God has taught that trials come to train us
So we with Christ eternally can reign.

Lord, give us strength to triumph in each trial—
With eyes above, keep serving you each day.
Keep teaching, God, that we can trust your wisdom
To bring us good through all that comes our way.

May we, dear Lord, complete the race you've given—
In faithfulness, rejoicing as we run
Until the day we see your face in glory
And hear you say, "It's finished, child! Well done!"
                                    —Jean Phillips

Bibliography

Zimbabwe: A Handbook, compiled by John House and Margaret and Beryl Salt (Harare, Zimbabwe: Mercury Press [Pvt.] Ltd., 1983).

Great Spaces Washed with the Sun, Members of the National Federation of Women's Institutes of Rhodesia (Salisbury, Rhodesia: M.O. Collins, (Pvt.) Ltd., 1967.

Ingrid Otto, *Christ On Trial in Zimbabwe-Rhodesia* (Pretoria, South Africa: The Dorothea Mission, 1979).

Colin Saunders, *Murray McDougall and the Story of Triangle* (Triangle, Rhodesia: Triangle Limited, 1977).

Dirk Scbwager, *Lesotho.* (Maseru, Lesotho: Schwager Publications, 1986).

Randy Sprinkle, *Until the Stars Appear.* (Birmingham, AL: New Hope, 1994).

The Rhodesia Literature Bureau, *The Bundu Book of Trees Flowers and Grasses.* (Salisbury, Rhodesia: Longmans of Rhodesia [Pvt.] Ltd., 1965).

The Rhodesia Literature Bureau, *The Bundu Book of Birds Insects and Snakes* (Salisbury, Rhodesia: Longmans of Rhodesia [Pvt.] Ltd., 1967).

Internet

<http://encarta.msn.com>, "Lesotho" from *Microsoft Encarta Online Encyclopedia 2000*, 1997-2000, Microsoft Corp.

<http://www.infoplease.com/ipa/A0107714.html>, "Lesotho" from The Columbia Electronic Encyclopedia, 1994, 2000, on Infoplease.com. 2001, The Learning Network Inc.

<http://www.infoplease.com/ipa/A0107983.html>, "South Africa" from *The Columbia Electronic Encyclopedia*, 1994, 2000, on Infoplease.com. 2001, The Learning Network Inc.

<http://www.infoplease.com/ipa/a0108169.html>, "Zimbabwe" from *The Columbia Electronic Encyclopedia*, 1994, 2000, on Infoplease.com. 2001, The Learning Network Inc.

Personal Papers

Jean Phillips, Personal letters, Newsletters, Emails and Reports to Rhodesia Baptist Mission and to Baptist Mission in Zimbabwe, 1956-1999.

Jean Jarvis, 1948,
missions volunteer

Jean's eight siblings in 1965: Bruce, Spurgeon,
Carol, Esther, Wilbur, Jean, Bonnie, and Dot.

Gene and Jean's wedding, 1952, with Jean's parents
and Gene's mother.

Gene baptizing at Samba Ranch, 1965. Jean and Rebecca wear the Baptist WMU uniform. John looks on.

Gene and Jean with Mark and John in Shabani, Rhodesia, 1958.

The church at Samba Ranch, 1966. Mark is out front to right.

Gene preaching in Triangle in 1966 in classroom where Runyararo (Peace) Church was begun. Paul, Jean, John, and Beth are present.

The interdenominational, multiracial crusade in the Murray McDougall School Hall, 1975. The Rev. John Broom is at front.

Jean and Rebecca
in Shabani, 1963

Beth, Jean, John, Gene, Paul, and Mark in
Triangle, 1966

Journeyman Tim Cearley with Rwokuda Jachi and other youth in
front of Runyararo Baptist Church, Triangle, 1975

On a visit to Sasame Mission Station in 1982, Jean views one of the former missionary residences, then in ruins as a result of the war.

Gene and Jean's house in 1986 with the beautiful garden God gave them. It was built on the same spot as the one in ruins.

Gene and Jean with Sasame neighbors and co-workers, Mary
Louise Clark and Wes and Laurie Wilcox, 1990

Jean teaching adult literacy at the Tsivi village, 1990

Jean with Journeymen Joseph and Denise Lugo and some of the pastors and wives in the Gokwe area, 1990

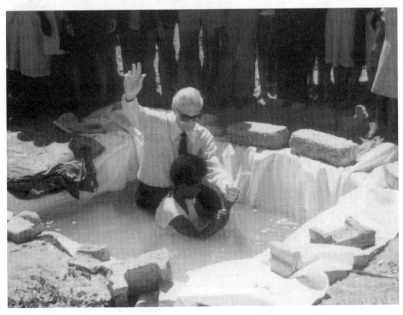

A baptismal service in the Gokwe area

Tent Meeting at Thabana Mohlomi, January, 1999.

Camping out, at right, at Thabana Mohlomi in front of where team stayed. Toyota Venture at right was later stolen.

After returning home to Morija after their abduction, Gene and Jean, below, with dog, Laurie.

Gene and Jean in the Lesotho mountains after release from kidnappers

Gene and Jean are welcomed at airport in Columbia, SC, by family
and friends, July, 1999. Son John embraces them as grandson
Danny looks on.

Family gathering, Thanksgiving, 1999: Front: Robin (on stool) and
Janice Phillips, Jean, Bethany Gestring, April Phillips, Jordan, Beth,
Michelle, and Wes Gestring. Back: John, Danny, and Mark Phillips,
Gene, Shana, Paul, and Michal.

Map of Zimbabwe

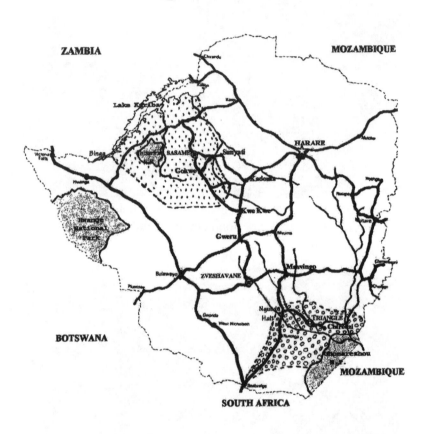

ZAMBIA

MOZAMBIQUE

BOTSWANA

SOUTH AFRICA

MOZAMBIQUE

KEY TO MAP

National Parks

☆ Capital & Place of Language Study 1956

◉ Places we lived 1957-95

Our Area 1964-84

Our Area 1984-95

▬ Roads

— Rivers

KEY TO NAME CHANGES AFTER 1980

Zimbabwe - Rhodesia
Harare - Salisbury
Masvingo - Fort Victoria
Zveshavane - Shabani
Gweru - Gwelo
Kwe Kwe - Que Que
Kadoma - Gatooma
Mutare - Umtali
Hwange - Wankie
Chinoyi - Sinoia

MAPS OF SOUTH AFRICA AND LESOTHO

These missions books are also available

Gleanings from God's Word by Gene and Jean Phillips. As a sequel to *Rescue*, retired missionaries Gene and Jean Phillips wrote this succinct and highly practical devotional book, which is ideal for today's busy lives, to help Christians read through the Bible in a year.

_____Copies at $12.95=_____

Beyond Surrender by Barbara J. Singerman. After surrendering to missions in Benin, Barbara Singerman and her family found that the only similarity between themselves and the Beninese that they all walk upright on two feet and smile. Why serve in a place where major diseases stalked their lives, where accomplishing basic, daily tasks caused unthinkable fatigue? The answer came in the desperate plea of villagers, "Please come back and tell us more about Jesus."

_____Copies at $12.95=_____

Unmoveable Witness by Marion Corley. An alarming interrogation by Colombia's version of the FBI. A dangerous mishap at a construction site. A frightening theft at his home in Bucaramanga, Colombia. What kept Marion and Evelyn Corley on the mission field for 22 years when others might have returned to Stateside comforts?

_____Copies at $9.95=_____

Awaken the Dawn by Doris B. Wolfe. Christian romance novel set in the jungles of South America involving two missionaries, one a recent widower with two children and the other a young, never-married single woman. He's a pilot. She's a teacher. Dramatic real-life situations test their faith.

_____Copies at $9.95=_____

Add $3.00 shipping for first book, plus 50-cents for each additional book.

Shipping & handling _____

Texas residents add 8.25% sales tax _____

TOTAL ENCLOSED_____

check _____ or credit card # _____ exp. date_____
(Visa, MasterCard, Discover, American Express accepted)

Name _____

Address _____ Phone _____

City _____ State _____ Zip _____

Email _____

**For postal address, phone number, fax number, email address
and other ways to order from Hannibal Books, see page 183**

How to order more copies of
Rescue

and obtain a free Hannibal Books catalog
FAX: 1-972-487-7960
Call: 1-800-747-0738
Email: hannibalbooks@earthlink.net
Write: Hannibal Books
P.O. Box 461592
Garland, Texas 75046
Visit: www.hannibalbooks.com

Number of copies desired _____

Multiply number of copies by $12.95 __X__$12.95_

Cost of books: $_____

Please add $3 for postage and handling for first book and add 50-cents for each additional book in the order.

Shipping $_____

Total order $_____

Mark method of payment:

check enclosed _____

Credit card# _____ exp. date_____

(Visa, MasterCard, Discover, American Express accepted)

Name _____

Address _____

City State, Zip _____

Phone _____ FAX _____

Email _____